The

Weekend Flyer

The
Weekend Flyer

Sixty-Five Years of Weekend Adventures
in the Cockpit

Mike Echo

CITI OF
BOOKS

CITIOFBOOKS, INC.
3736 Eubank NE Suite A1
Albuquerque, NM 87111-3579
www.citiofbooks.com
Hotline: 1 (877) 389-2759
Fax: 1 (505) 930-7244

Ordering Information:
Quantity sales. Special discounts are available on quantity purchases by corporations, associations, and others. For details, contact the publisher at the address above.

Printed in the United States of America.

| ISBN-13: | Softcover | 979-8-89391-013-1 |
| | eBook | 979-8-89391-014-8 |

Library of Congress Control Number: 2024914628

For the IAF

And My Beloved Wife, Mary

For Enriching My Life

So Much

Table of Contents

INTRODUCTION

The Weekend Flyers

This is a love story of people who have a passion for flying or following aviation in its many forms. Some are enthusiasts practicing their passion for flying or learning to fly. Mostly recreationally, on weekends. This occupation requires dedication and much time and resources to achieve the utmost of the activity. For me,it was the flying itself, exploring, investigating, and analyzing other pilots' unique experiences. l have been doing this for over sixty years, and my work has been published in many aviation publications as well as in TV programs around the world. I owned two gliders and a Mooney and flew on over forty different aircraft. Yet, for me, life did not revolve around flying alone. I was extremely busy in my various businesses over many decades. Yet, always found time for this other passion.

On that journey, I met very special people, huge achievers, and unique human beings. Almost anyone can fly a plane, but only a few may be outstanding. Most air forces choose the few and the best of their citizens to join their militaries as pilots and even fewer as fighter pilots.

Professional vs. "Recreational"

Many times, I hear people referring to General Aviation (GA) pilots as "amateurs" or "hobbyists" only because this group does not, or no longer, fly for pay, as opposed to "Professionals."

These references are wrong and must be removed from aviation's vocabulary. All pilots must be professionals if they wish to survive the experience. The aircraft does not care who flies it. If the pilot is careless, sloppy, or reckless, the plane will sooner or later bite, no matter what ticket he or she holds-all must strive to get to a top level of proficiency and flying professionalismcommercial or private.

All flying involves a lifetime of learning, training, studying, and upgrading, not only about technically flying an aircraft,. but all must also be thoroughly familiar with the mechanics, the systems of the aircraft they fly, aerodynamics rules, weather, and the laws in the environment they fly. Naturally, experience plays a big role; fly, fly, fly.

Once again, there is no room for amateurs in flying; *all* pilots must be equally professionals.

My Introduction to Aviation

I was first introduced to flying at the age of seventeen and a half. At that age, I was enlisted in mandatory military service and arrived at the military's recruitment center for four weeks of rigorous examinations of every kind, from physical condition to phycological aptitude and whatnot. The conditions at the camp were just awful for a young teenager coming from a warm home. The treatment of the recruits by the low-level personnel was humiliating, and the food was even worse.

At the end of that period, a young Air Force recruitment officer approached me. "You were found to be suitable for service as aircrew in the Air Force. Would you agree to volunteer?" In those days, one was required to volunteer for flight School training, and in my underage case, I had to bring my parents' permission too. Realizing my hesitation, he suggested we first go and visit an Air Force base where the academy was located and defer my decision until then. I reluctantly agreed, knowing my mother would never offer her consent.

It was lunchtime at the base when we arrived, and the genteel officer suggested: "Let's go and have lunch." We entered the cadets' mess hall, and I could not believe my eyes; servers were waiting ondiners with porcelain plates, silverware, and a choice of menu. That was my tipping point. On that day,I was introduced to aviation-the bout with my mother was another story.

So, everyone's flying gets their introduction in some different way. My own was through the military, but there are many programs in the USA and elsewhere in the form of youth flying dubs and flight schools accepting members at a very early age. Also, there are flight schools in almost every airport that would accept students of all ages-as it is never too late to learn to fly.

You learn by making mistakes, which is if they are not too serious about scaring you. But then you alsolearn that recovering from a scary one properly is gratifying. Yet, making some contro, I mistakes are one thing but entering bad weather or flying recklessly is another. Entering bad weather is anact of bad judgment, and it is not very friendly to aviation. Pilots are avid students of weather phenomena and current conditions en route planned for flying.

There are two primary rules of flying: Visual Flight Rules (VFR) and Instrument Flight Rules (IFR). The first requires *visual conditions*, which, among others, the pilot is required to fly within a certain distance from clouds, vertically and horizontally, and with good forward visibility. IFR Rules require the pilot to be certified for Instrument Flying in weather that requires flying under such rules. The flight is performed using the instruments on the panel as references without relying on physical vision of the environment around the plane. The newer planes are equipped with advanced navigation, synthetic vision, electronic maps, radar, and many ways of getting information in the air (including music) necessary for a safe flight.

Solo Flights

I did my first solo in a Piper J-3 Cub. This light plane was manufactured by Piper Aircraft between 1938 and 1940. Flying the Cub was a delight. While it was slow at approx. 80 MPH, flying it low and slow was quite exciting. I was required to be ready for a solo flight after some 10-12 hours of instructions. The Cub was quite a challenge for a first-time teenage flyer, as we were required, by standards of that time, to land it on three points (two main and one back gear) simultaneously. I proudly soloed after only 7 hours. Yet, in civil aviation, there is no rush, and every new pilot takes her or his time to achieve that goaI.

Every pilot remembers his or her first solo flight forever. Even after flying in some forty different aircraft through the years, I will never forget my solo flight in the Cub. It was a physical as well as an emotional reward that I gladly lived through. When you have full control of your movements in three dimensions for the first time, it certainly affects your confidence, as well as your selfesteem, profoundly. In my Wings Project (see Giving

Back page 145), we, as volunteers, managed to turn someliterally criminal teenagers, into abiding and productive citizens, only by improving their self-esteem, affording them control of their craft and self, as an alternative to controlling other people through criminal activity. Many of these teenagers (now adults) are still communicating with us. I could not have granted these young humans such an opportunity if I did not experience and been impacted by it myself.

I tried to keep stories that I either experienced myself or those I could personally replicate in the manner that they were told to me. Especially when describing pilots' war experiences, it was done with the purpose of repeating the situations, comparing the adversary crafts and men technicallyfor the performance of a like aircraft in peacetime. That, of course, did not include my own flying experiences. Sometimes, a warbird described here is no longer available for a test flight, so I had to be satisfied with how the story was told to me by the pilot.

CHAPTER ONE
THE BUZZ, REVISITED

This Saturday morning is nothing special. As always, I got up early for my morning workout, and the first thing I do after getting out of bed is look up and out the window. It's early October, the temperature's warm, and the air is calm. The sky is covered 'wall to wall' with thick dark clouds. Looks like another chore's day at home. By about ten-thirty, the sky's still dark looking, and the forecast hasno promise for anything better for the rest of the day. I decide against the chores anyway and start towards the airport, where I have been spending the past few Saturdays searching for memories of days long past.

The airport is a small private one in the middle of a country farm some seventy miles northwest of New York City. The field is nothing more than a few old buildings in desperate need of repair and a paved runway. The sign announcing the establishment is so old that the writing is faded almost beyond legibility. Housing the local FBO, as well as the kind of makeshift hangar/storage, is a long, low, and narrow old structure on its last leg. Yet, besides its resemblance to Kitty-Hawk, this airport does have something special about it.

I found it on the Internet, and back in August took a ride up there to check out the local soaring club. There was a barrage of air machines scattered everywhere. Old and new, experimental and vintage planes were commingled side by side with colorful hot-air balloons, hang gliders, and slick sailplanes. The place was humming with activity. "A playground for grownups," I noted, not without amusement.

I took my first flight when II was just about fourteen or fifteen years old. It was on a glider. That flight was years later, followed by a solo. The sensation of a first flight and the emotions evoked on one's first flight with every pilot telling you are forever captured and carved deep in a pilot's memory. I would best describe it as the ultimate feeling of freedom, an excitement filled with wholesomeness, elation, and delight. Ever since then, I have flown many militaries and general aviation airplanes, never to recapture that first flight/first-solo buzz.

At the airport, I find some of the boys hanging around, trying to make up their minds about whether it's worth taking off into this dismal sky. "It's a good day for practice," says Hank in his deep assertive voice. Andrew shakes his head and mumbles, 11 1 should really be trying out my newcanopy." Meanwhile, it clears just a bit, and those black clouds are now scattered about the grayish-blue sky. "What do you think?" I pose to Bob. Bob, who I example to everyone's favorite uncle and who would always favor the sunny side of an encounter, replies: "It sure doesn't look like much, but if you like, I will ride out with you." 11 Let's go," I propose.

We take the orange Schweitzer 2-33. "What would you like me to do?" asks Bob as we're being towed out. "Nothing," I answer, "enjoy the ride," and release at 2500 indicated. As soon as we are released over the northeast side of the airport, the audio-vario starts shrieking like mad, and it would not cease for almost the entire duration of this 55 minutes flight. We hit a strong thermal that keeps taking us up.

Andrew, who's meanwhile also airborne, detected action by us and has now joined us in working the thermal. He's flying some fifty feet below us at about 4500. Hank too, who was riding with Jason, rushed to join the party and is now circling some five hundred feet below. The scene is breathtaking, and emotions are flying high inside the cockpit. I see Andrew almost eye to eye, circling below in his streamline silver and blue Schweitzer 2-35, the yellow bulky 2-33 way down with Hank and Jason spiraling upward, and in between, soaring in a tight circle, almost motionless, are a couple of hawks; wings spread out. "Soaring with the eagles," I whisper in wonder.

This is my closest recital with nature. Caressed by its gentle forces, harmonious with its elements, free as a bird.

This was my reintroduction to my first flight, my first solo, many years ago.

CHAPTER TWO
CHALLENGE IN THE DESERT

Once you have tasted flight, you will walk the earth with your eyesturned skywards, for there you have been, and there you will longtreturn.

Leonardo da Vinci

Of all the aircraft I have flown recreationally, I favor gliders the most.

It's a couplie of months since I rediscovered soaring, and I've accumulated some 30 hours of glider time. I'm curious and anxious to know and experience more about this unique form of flight, and I'm ready for more excitement.

The ultimate in gliding is cross-country soaring. I've heard stories of flights--out and return, fora thousand kilometers (roughly 621 miles), and 500 km and 300 km are even more common - but it's still quite incomprehensible to me. I'm wondering if I can catch a glimpse of that experience.

A glider is essentially an airplane without an engine. It's designed to minimize drag (anything that resists smooth airmass penetration) and to maximize lift (the force that pushes it up). Nevertheless, to stay up, favorable atmospheric conditions must prevail, and the pilot's skills are also an essential factor.

Minden, Nevada, I've been told, is the U.S. Mecca of soaring. Nestled in a valley at the foot of the towering Sierra Nevada Mountains, the airfield is some 4,500 ft above sea level. It enjoys unusual thermal activity in the hot Nevada summer and tremendous mountain winds (known as Mountain Waves) in the fall and spring.

I called one of the local glider operators at Minden/Tahoe airport and asked what kind of experience! would need to fly their gliders. I'm told that with my "poweru background, 50 hours would suffice if I passed a check ride. While I have a good number of power-time, I hardly have any gliders experience, and thus, I'm quite apprehensive about being rejected. So, I lie and tell them I have the minimum required.

I did a little more research and determined that the best time to go would be in July, only a couple of weeks ahead. I call Minden again and buy a seven-day package in a Discus A, a highperformance single-seat glider, somewhat more advanced yet, already lagging behind the fast-advancing technology. The package includes unlimited flight hours and a couple of tows to 2,500 ft above ground level (AGL) each day.

My fascination with gliders goes back many years. When I was fourteen, I belonged to an Air Force-sponsored youth flying club. We spent most of our time building gliders and other aircraft models and learning the rules responsiblefor the amazing phenomenon of flight. We've even been flown a couple of times in twin-seat, open-cockpit gliders. It was an experience I never forgot.

The time had come to go to Minden. I show up bright and early. There is no one on the field to greet me yet. The air is still and deads quiet. Sandy desert hills in the distance are awash in the bright rising sun. There is the sharp scent of earth, still damp from the morning dew, hanging in the air. The Sierra Mountains, a few miles to the west, cast their awesome shadows onto the valley. I'm standing out there, engaging all my senses and absorbing the awe of nature.

At about 11:00 hour, George, my check-ride instructor, and I jump into a two-seater Grobe-103 and get towed to 6,500 ft above sea level (MSL), approximately 2,000 ft AGL. Upon release from the tow plane, I caught a strong thermal that took us up to about 9,000 ft and a short while after to 11,000. I'm astonished by the amount of lift all around us. We stay out for about an hour playing in the sky and exploring the valley before George calls the check-ride concluded, and we return for landing. "You can go up again in the 103 or take the single-seat 102, but don't leave the valley!" he says. "Wow ... " I think while preparing the G-102 for the solo flight.

I spent over four hours in the air, dazzled by the awesome scenery. The towering Alp-like Sierra Nevada range, with its snow-capped Mount Paterson and White Mountain to the west, Nutmeg Mountain, and the far-flung desert to the east. Breathtaking. I never imagined it would be this easy, I reflect as I land back at the field.

Exhausted but fulfilled, I go to bed replaying the events of the day and thinking impatiently of tomorrow.

Day two .. Andy, a senior instructor at the FBO (Fixed Base Operator), approaches me as I check the weather conditions for the day. "Would you like to do some cross-country flying?"he asks. "Sure," I enthusiastically responded. "Then, let's leave immediately." He says, "The weather is perfect." We grab oxygen gear and GPS navigation equipment, then get a ride to the twin Grobe.

Andy is a man in his forties .. He's spent most of his life around airplanes and gliders and has the reputation of being a superb pilot, a fiercely competitive contestant, and as reckless as they come--the sort of pilot more typical of WWII than modern aviation.

It's mid-morning; the wind is from the southwest at 10 to 15 MPH. Cumulus clouds are already everywhere, organized in long lines following the wind direction. The temperature on the ground is around 85° F, and the dew point is about 3°F. This would put the cloud base, or top of the thermals, at an incredible 18,000 ft, plus or minus.

A thermal is what gliders use to climb and stay aloft. It's a mass of the air - a bubble warmer than its surroundings that, obeying the laws of physics, continues to rise until it cools to the temperature of the prevailing dew point. The dew point is the temperature at which the air, with sufficient humidity, condenses. The air (and thermals) typically lose heat at a lapse rate of approximately 3°F per 1,000 ft. When it reaches the dew point, clouds form. To estimate the size of a thermal (or cloud base), you take the surface temperature (in this case 85°F) and subtractthe dew point (30°F), multiply that sum by 1000 ft and then divide the result by the lapse rate (3°F). Today, the cloud base would calculate to an impressive 18,333 ft. The wider the spread, the higher the cloud base would be. A glider (or a bird) circling within this air mass could climb from close to the ground -level right up to the 18,000 cloud-based or beyond. Depending on the temperature and humidity, the air may continue to rise quite violently into the cloud and up to some very high altitudes. The conditions inside the cloud are hostile and extremely hazardous to all aircraft, small or large.

I climb into the front seat while Andy takes the back. I'm wearing shorts, a T-shirt, sneakers, and a hat to protect my head from the blazing Nevada sun-standard gliding gear. "You are not wearing a hat?" I claim. "Nope," Andy replies and adds, "I'm a living cancer experiment." I shrug and continue setting up the equipment... wondering whether he'd be using oxygen at altitude.

A tow plane lines up in front, preparing to pull. us up to about 6,000 ft, some 2,000 ft above the ground. It's hot as hell inside the glider, and I'm eager to take off into higher, cooler air. "During the flight, I'll point out some spots where thermals typically form," Andy says. "Great, thank you." I could mark these locations on my charts and use the information for future flights. As Andy and I discussed, we're going to attempt three points, 300 KM flight. The tow liine is hitched to the twin, and I signal OK to the line boy and tow pilot. We are pulled along the runway, rotate, and begin climbing toward the predetermined release point.

I release the glider from the tow plane and start circling inside the "home" thermal. Thethermals are strongerthan any I've ever experienced, with vertical speed exceeding 1000 ft per minute. After the initial thermal that takes us to almost 18,000 ft, we head almost directly southwest until we merge with a northeasterner cloud street, leading straight into the desert. Clouds that are organized along the wind direction are known in the soaring world as Cloud Streets. Under a cloud street, gliders can fly in a straight line at high speed.Depending on the strength of the thermals' vertical speed, they fly along them without losing any altitude. The way it works is that whilst the thermal pulls the glider up and towards the cloud, the pilot resists it by pushingthe glider's nose downward, using a gravity vector to turn the vertical pull into a forwarding motion. The greater the vertical speed, the greater can become the forward speed in leveled flight. Cloud streets are known for stretching out for hundreds of miles.

We've flown the same cloud street for some 170 km (approx. 105 miles), racing at an indicated airspeed of about 120 knots ... and still going. Staying, for al I that long, in the shade of the clouds, I begin to feel the 3°F outside temperature. Meanwhile, I sense the smell of cigarette smoke merging from the back seat-we are both breathing pure oxygen, and the mix of oxygen, fire, and suntan oil is a deadly combination, making us a fast-moving bomb under the cloud. "Watch that the cloud doesn't swallow us," says Andy. Makes me wonder; what will kill me first, the cloud or the second-hand smoke...

After some 125 miles under the clouds, we break northwest towards Silver Ranch, a dry lake forty miles east of Reno's Class C terminal. The sky now turns mostly bilue, with some local clouds scattered in the distance, marking possible active thermals. We reached Tiger Junction just in time to connect with a strong thermal that would bring us back up to 15,000 ft (approx. 10,000 AGL) after losing most of the altitude we had cruising towards a disappointing Cu over Silver Ranch from the safety of the cloud street. At Tiger, we are approximately twenty miles north of Silver Ranch and 80 miles from home. With no additional lift and in ideal conditions, the glider would take us some 65 miles before we hit the ground.

It's now late afternoon, thermals are scarce, and those still around have gone much weaker. We are rushing southwest towards Carson City (and Minden) to make it before we lose all the remaining lifts still in the sky. While I estimate we could reach Carson City, there is no way we could make Minden unless we stumble upon a super thermal-we may need to land out somewhere in the desert... We find no thermals and continue to steadily lose altitude... although the palm of my hands begins to perspire, I'm not yet concerned, even with the prospect of spending much of the night on some remote desert hill, waiting for the retrieve. Andy is completely silent. Carson City gets closer, and I find a weak, 50-100 ft/min thermal that brings us up to about 2,000 ft AGL... but no more. I start planning to land at Carson City airport. "No matter what you do, don't try and land at Dayton Valley. Not very friendly people," Andy suddenly snaps. "I'm planning for Carson City. We may be able to make it "direct" to runway 27," I reply. "O...kaay," he mutters and contacts Carson City Tower to announce our arrival-gliders do have landing priority over powered aircraft. We arrive with sufficient altitude to enter a modified pattern, and I land the glider at the very beginning of the runway to allow enough room for the retrieving tow plane to pick us up and conclude the flight in Minden, twenty-two miles to the south.

That was quite a thrilling experience for me, and despite the premature landing, we managed to complete almost 200 miles--Little that I know what is yet in store for me tomorrow. I thank Andy for a great flight and head straight to the sack.

Day three. I show up at the airport bright and early and check out the weather on a soaring website servicing this location-it looks like another good soaring day, and I think perhaps I'd hang close-by flying within the confine of the valley. But no, Andy has another plan.

"How did you like yesterday's flight," he opens.

"It was awesome, you know it," I reply.

"Well then, how about a three-glider cross-country formation flight? I already spoke to Pat. She would like to join us," he says without waiting for my confirmation and calls Pat to join the briefing.

"We are going up to plus minus 17,500 ft, 500 ft below our Class A floor limit, and we'll meet at Pine Nut to form our three-glider formation. I will lead. Mike, you'll fly the Mini-Nimbus, Pat the LS-4, and I'll load the G-102 with water to keep up with your gliders' superior performance ...

Let's go."

Wow, isn't that exciting? I'm thinking. The idea of flying formations, some half a mile apart, increases the chances of connecting with a thermal! along the way by at least one of us. When the lift is detected, the others join into a circle and gain altitude together.

"When I announce on the radio the codeword 'kindergarten,' we all switch to 123.475, a frequency we can use exclusively," Andy instructs.

"Sounds like a plan," I announce, and Pat confirms.

We get our equipment, and this time I make sure I have a flight logger to record all aspects of my flight for future reference and scrutiny.

It's amazing, I recollect, that only a few years ago, GPS was virtually unknown in General or Commercial Aviation, much less in gliders. Today's loggers (or flight recorders) record everything the aircraft performs, from directions of flight, maneuvers, the number of thermals, attempted and/or flown to altitudes and distances, all in 2-second intervals. The data gets analyzed for the pilot in almost unlimited variations and then displayed on any PC in a variety of three-dimensional maps, statistical charts, time-condensed animated depictions, and more.

I'm well rested, ready for this adventure, yet quite excited with anticipation. It is about 11:00 h when we're seated in our gliders. The temperature is already blazing at almost 100°F, the remote launching stage is dead-quiet, and everything's at a standstill, bar the occasional dust devil and rolling tumbleweeds.

Andy takes off first, followed by me, and lastly, Pat gets launched. I get lucky, and upon release, I find a thermal that, within minutes, brings me up to the assigned altitude, waiting for Pat and Andy to catch up. Soon after, Andy announces being at the altitude. Pat is struggling, and Andy and I continue to circle for at least twenty more minutes, waiting for her. Meanwhile, the lift at the upper deck is almost unlimited. I stay over Pine Nut, trying hard to stay below 18,000 ft.

I can see Pat joining the rendezvous just when she announces her arrival. Andy takes the lead and Pat and I will follow at Andis at four and eight o'clock, respectively.

We're flying straight southeast along the Sierra Nevada range, over Flying Mouse Top towards Mount Paterson, and then turn northeast towards Sweetwater Strip.

The scenery is just breathtaking over the 14,000 ft peaks. Over Sweetwater, we bump into a strong thermal and make a few circles to gain a couple of thousand feet or so before turning southwest again. At this point, we've been traveling for 03:17 hours; we are at 17,700 ft and approx. 106 miles from home. Below is the Nevada desert with no sign of civilization in sight. This is when Andy announces our return.

"We are going back home. Follow me."

I feel quite confident and respond with, "I'm going for another 50 miles to complete 300 miles out and return. I will advise when turning back north."

"OK, Mike, follow us when you're done."

I'm committed and far from home over hostile terrains. I'm on my own...

I fly straight for about twenty-two more miles and down to about 9,000 over ground level. I figure I will need to climb to about 13,000 to clear the mountains and about 24,000 feet, accumulatively, to reach Minden just when I realize that the lift over the valley has weakened considerably and is actually diminishing.

Concern starts lingering in, and I decide to turn back with no further delay. I fly back for about 30miles without a slight detection of lift.

My glider is dropping in altitude, as does my trembling heart. Now the mountains look tall above us.

I'm reaching a ridge some ten miles west of Hilton Ranch.

Hilton Ranch, elevation 495 ft, is owned by the famous Barron Hilton. Hilton, a glider pilot himself, uses the M Flying Ranch to fly his gliders in this remote desert retreat. Years later, it would be known as the departing point of adventurer Steve Fossett before the desert crash that took his life. It is also known for its bi-annual Hilton Cup, a week-long competition of cross-country gliding. The story goes that a glider pilot forced to land out at the ranch will be treated to a sandwich, ice cream, and a tow back to altitude.

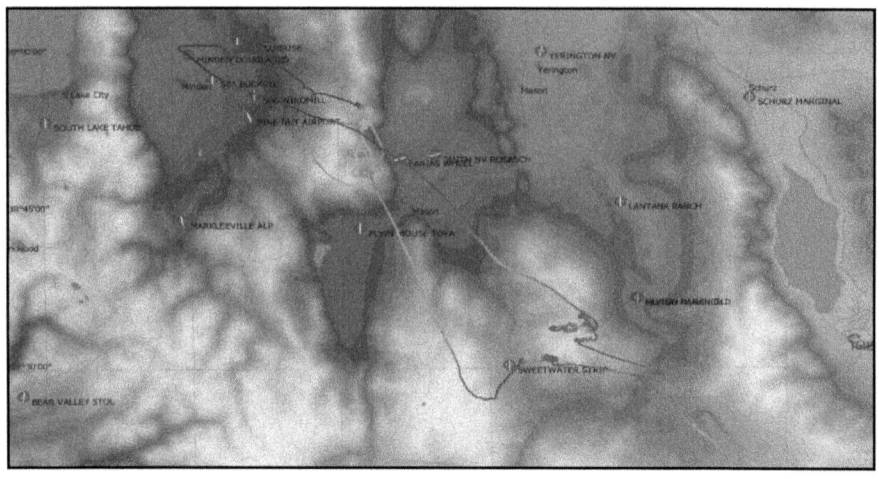

I'm low. I estimate less than 1000 ft over the bottom of that ridge and the rugged terrain. Sweetwater is at approximately 6900 ft elevation. I need to climb some 5,000 feet to get there. For now, all I see is the rocks below me and on the slope leading high up this huge mountain. So, Sweetwater is out of the question, but Hilton Ranch may still be an option.

"How're you doing, Mike?" I hear Andy on the radio.

"Two thousand feet," I responded.

"You're going down! What's your position?" he adds.

"Eight to ten miles west of Hilton Ranch," I report.

"Go for the ice cream or land in the valley and stay there for the night. Be careful."

I hit a small bump. Its lift! Tiny, but still some upward movement, 'not going down so quickly, Andy,' I'm thinking.

"Will advise," I radio back.

I know that by now, they're all at Minden and in the air, listening with anticipation.

I lower the volume and focus on flying my machine.

My vertical speed is between 30 to 50 fpm, and I'm circling very close to the cliff, where that little lift is. My wingtips are only inches away from the rock. I can't help but imagine fiberglass debris piling up down the bottom of the cliff any moment now.

I'm intensely focused on flying my glider at high angles of attack, steep banks, and constantly at the glider1 s stall speed to remain in the crucially needed tight circle inside that baby bubble of rising air. I don't recall ever having to apply this much concentration flying any maneuver in any aircraft and for this length of time. The heat inside my cockpit is just as intense as the tension inside every one of my muscles. But physically, I feel neither.

I once participated in an open-sea swim contest. The task was a mile out and return. I was a very young and pretty good swimmer. I swam vigorously outbound, but halfway back, I got exhausted wrestling with the waves and currents-I thought I would drown. My head was sporadically submerged in the water in total exhaustion. Suddenly, and in a matter of a quick trice, I found myself in a state of unmitigated concentration and complete focus on my survival. My vigor returned, and my newly found energy carried me back. I don't recall elements of that last phase. I just remember landing safely on the beach.

My wrestle with this fledgling thermal brings me back to that swimming contest years ago in the Mediterranean.

2,100 feet! Here's another kick in the butt. I bank sharply towards the center of the thermal. It's getting stronger ... 2,600 feet. Vertical speed is now averaging 350 FPM. Wow, perhaps this little guy is my saver! I circle steadily, extremely coordinated at or near the yet higher stall speed. I gain altitude at an even pace. 4,800 feet! 5,200; 6,000; and ... climbing.

The rocks look smaller now and further away. At 16:41 hour local, I'm at 10,000. "How's it going, Mike?" Andy inquires.

"11,000," I snap.

"That-a-boy, that-a-boy," exclaims Andy, not without relief.

By 17:00, I'm at 17,990 feet. I gained the top 7,000 feet within 11 minutes and 16,000 feet within 40.

"At 18,000 feet and heading home," I announce on the radio. "That-a-boy," comes the answer.

I breathe freely. lt1 s much cooler up here, the sun is setting in the west, and I feel quite relaxed cruising at 110 knots straight home. I figure, with the altitude, I can reach Minden without circling at all.

At 17:26:28 h, I land on runway 30 at Minden.

Duration: 5 hours 12 minutes (and 24 seconds); total distance 259.2 miles; average speed: 71 knots and the mood... still up there at 18 thousand.

This article was first published in AOPA on line and other international aviation magazines.

CHAPTER THREE
CLOSING THE CIRCLE

"Bullfighting is the only art in which the artist is in danger of death and in which thedegree of brilliance in the performance is left to the fighter's honor."

Ernst Hemingway

He felt strange, tensed, and mystified. A quiver went down his spine as he looked at his old adversary straight and up close. He knew well how canny, how swift, and how powerful it was. He recalled how many times he put his very life to the test in confrontations. He was now about to shake an appeasing hand of an old and familiar enemy ...

Ret. Brigadier General Giora (Epstein) Even is an IAF living legend. Despite twice being rebuffed from joining the Air Force, and no less from joining a combat squadron, he made his way to do just that and turned out to be the Air Force's most revered fighter pilot and legendary as both a superb pilot and a fierce fighter. Dozens of times, he was called to intercept enemy aircraft, and seventeen of them, a world record uncontested by anyone for more than forty years, made him fall off the sky. "There were too many of them in the combat arenas, and as long as I had sufficient fuel and armaments, I had to continue and fight," says Even.

And on his own account of single combat on October 20, 1973, tells it all:

I am assigned aircraft 561, a Nesher on loan from squadron 113. I notice my Number Two and the rest of my quartet merge into the taxiway as we keep radio silence. We taxi towards the end of runway 271 where we will begin our roflout. Although the temperatures are not the usual desert-scorching highs, it's quite warm inside the cockpit, and the anticipation is even higher. I may never return from this mission. My wife and kids may never see me again. But I deal with that fact the way I do with .any other data; this time, I push the thoughts away. I have no fear, never had. I have known no fear since childhood; of course, the absence of this built-in alert is a flaw, and I attempt to compensate for it with an intense focus on my skills and with an uncompromising knowledge of my equipment.

We line up on the runway while revving our engines and take off with a thundering roar. Forming an orderly formation, we turn slightly left to approximately 230°, heading toward the Great Bitter lake, about halfway south of the Suez Canal.

Today is Saturday, October 20, fourteen days since the war has begun and my third day back from Headquarters. My wife and kids are still with my parents. They went there for the Holiday and stayed after the war broke out. It's a beautiful late afternoon. The sky is blue, with moderate temperatures on the ground and visibility as far as the eye can see. I just managed to escape a desk job, and my spirit is high. I'm back at my squadron, and I already have four Sukhoi kills to my credit from yesterday's scramble. Psychologically, I'm all set for more action.

We arrive at the lake but see no enemy planes. Control insists that they are there. I can usually spot bogies from a great distance. Ah, here they are. I spot a pair of MiG-21 about twenty-four miles away, southwest of the lake. They are cruising north at about 20,000 ft of altitude, northwest of us. I announce, "bogies in sight," lift the cover, and throw the weapons-activation switch up while unfolding the gun's trigger on the stick to its ready position. I dump my drop tanks,, break to the right toward them, and glance to verify that the others in my formation are following suit. As I lead towards the rear of the cruising MiGs, the horizon is suddenly filled with approaching MiG-21s--ten or twelve pairs--maneuvering into combat positions against the four of us. It's a trap. The single pair was the bait, and the sharks were hiding down below. We simply didn't see them, and neither did Air One.

As I go after Number Two of the 'baiting pair' and blow him with a missile, I hear my own Number Two, Edres, report that he's leaving the formation to take on another pair; I continue to chase the leader, who tries hard to outmaneuver me.

Edres makes a sharp right-turn to position himself well within his missile's optimum tracking angle and launches. Due to the sharp turn his Shafrir missile has passed close to the fuselage, which emits the blazing rocket fumes into his engine's air-intake and causes a compressor stall. His victim, though, is eliminated. I order Edres to leave for home. As I am maneuvering behind my own prey, I see Geva, another one of my pilots, chasing a MiG into the distance. He shoots it down but goes after it so far that he can't find hjs way back to the combat arena and returns home.

For three to four minutes, I'm still after the leader, who turned out to be the ambush planner. He's trying to evade me using every maneuver in the book: loops, inverted flights, sharp turns, split Ss, rolls, and whatnot.

rm right behind him, pulling Gs that would knock a rock unconscious. Meanwhile, the fourth Mirage in our foursome reports his own kill. He has run out of fuel, and he, too, has also gone home. The chase brings the two of us to less than 3,000 feet, and that crazy pilot attempts his craziest maneuver yet. At that low altitude, he pulls a Split S,. makes half a roll onto his back,. and pulls back towards the ground. Slowing the aircraft with everything he's got he is hoping to recover before he hits the ground. Quick glances outside the cockpit and at my altimeter help me decide not to follow this dangerous move, and I break to the left and down to cut him off at the exit (presuming he survives the stunt). I watch him exiting the Sat zero altitudes, raising a huge cloud of dust. I'm sure he crashed, but seconds later, he emerges majestically from his own dust cloud, at an almost vertical attitude,. shooting out a huge column of fire from its fully deployed backburner. But he's too slow at the exit, and that's when I get him, with a short burst of my cannons. I feel for the man. He was a fighter. My heart misses a beat when I swing back and discover a 21 riding my tail and nine more all around.

Oil painting by Roy Grinnell of Epstein's IAI Nesher 561

on the October 20, 1973, air combat

We started with a one-to-six ratio, but now it's me, on my own, against the ten of them. And they"re waiting for me to get myself into one of their sights. r,No way, Hussein," I grumble. 'Tit fight you all. One MiG at a time." I'm excited and alert as adrenalin streams into my blood and into *every part of me. Eyes wide open; taking short breaths, I scan the sky for my prey. I know that with their inferior Atoll AA-2 missiles, they'll have to line up within 11° of my six o'clock to get me. Fortunately, this can only be done one at a time. I'm in defensive mode, letting them get behind me but looking for an opportunity to reverse positions swiftly. My angle-of-attack warning lights show solid red as I perform endless maneuvers in a very slow flight. l shake the one at my tail with a sharp break and turn towards another, finding myself face-to-face with two new MiGs. They simultaneously launch missiles at me and buzz a couple of feet above my head. All that's left for me to do is instinctively dunk inside the cockpit. I know the Atolls haven't the least chance of exploding at that close of a range--and never head-on--but I'm still concerned about damage to my canopy by a direct hit. The excitement of bottle fills the airwaves. Everyone in the War Room, at the squadron, Operations, and on the frequency is listening in. Announcements of kills, warnings,, reports, directions, and guidance are heard almost constantly. I look behind to find the next pair. Its leader is on my tail with his Number Two following right behind. I brake sharply to the left and beg;n a slow barrel ron delicately pulling· my throttle back as I squeeze my thumb on the speed-brake switch and stick-and-rudder in a coordinated roll, letti'ng him pass. I end the roll behind him and right on his tail, then bring him b,etween my diamonds and squeeze. The MiG explodes so close thatfragments of its fuselage fly by from all directions. I look beh;nd and notice that, except for one last pair, there are no other MiGs in sight. They enter, and I break to the right. They turn away and pull up. I pull up after them. When I am perpendicular, I take my shot and hit Number Two at his cockpit. The pilot does not eject. At that point, his Number One decides to run. I turn towards him at an ideal angle and launch. The missile passes right underneath him without exploding. "I don't believe it!u I mutter, "They didn't give me one of those ancient 9Hs?v I'll never find out what happened to that missile, but I missed the fifth kill in that battle. I have 800 liters and 30 shells in each cannon--enough for a couple more local dogfights but not near enough for a long chase at a 350-Hter per minute burn rate. So, I Jet him go. The radio is now silent. I call Control and report enough fuel and ammunition for additional targets. The crisp voice of the controller comes back: "No targets in the air, return to base." The sun begins to set on the western horizon painting a backdrop of crimson and gray up above. I cruise towards the airbase, land, and then taxi back to my den. I shut down the engine, turn the switches off, release my harness, and open the canopy to the breeze of the open air. My G-suit is soaking-wet with perspiration. Any attempts to stand up failed... My legs refuse to respond to my brain's command, spent from the intense physical stress of battle. I glance at the G-meter to find both needles stuck at the very end of each scale-way beyond their limits.*

Joe Gano is a friend living in Wilmington, Delaware, USA. Joe is a retired USAF Captain, an F-102 fighter pilot of the sixties, and now a successful businessman; he owns a little fleet of Soviet-era fighter jets, including a couple of MiG-21s and MiG-23, SU-25, L-39, L-29, and others. When I told him about Giora, he immediately extended an invitation for Giora to fly on the 21. "I am curious as to what Even th'inks of the MiG after flying against it for so long," he said. "I will arrange it," I replied. I spoke to Giera, and a couple of months later, we were all able to find a suitable time for the occasion. It is a beautiful early-October day in Wilmington. Temperatures are in the mid-seventies, scattered clouds at 71 000 ft, and the wind are blowing from the northwest at 5 to 8 knots. Everyone's gathered at the airport for the occasion. My wife and I arrived the night before with Giora and his wife, Sarah. Joe, the ground crew, and a couple of close friends met us there. The air was charged with anticipation, and the mix of all-aviator participants and spectators made for great chemistry. The crew and friends were elated to meet a famous Israeli Ace.

The delta-winged Mikoyan-Gurevich MiG-21UM model is the fighter-trainer equivalent of the MiG-21MF, designated Fishbed-J by NATO. Both were manufactured in the Czech Republic by order of the Soviet Air Force. The 21MF has 14,550 pounds of thrust and a weight of 16,610 lbs. (0.875 T /W ratios), including internal fuel. It is twice supersonic with a maximum speed of 1,353 MPH and wing loading of some 87.5 llbs./SF. Its service ceiling is an impressive 58,000 ft, with an amazing climb rate of 36,900 ft/min. In combat gear, it is armed with one twin-barrel 23mm cannon and two Atoll AA-2 air-to-air missiles.

It may appear crude, but it's a tough aircraft, designed to operate from rough fields and unfinished strips almost anywhere. The composition of its hardened exterior was, for years, an unsolved mystery for the west. Although it lacks the finesse of an American or French fighter, it certainly looks very intimidating.

Gearing up. Giora walks toward the aircraft, which is parked just outside of the dispatch office. Heart pounding, he never imagined this meeting would ever take place. The moment evokes the October 20 combat with some mixed feelings. The battle that destroyed more than half an Egyptian MiG-21 squadron, commanded by Gameel al- Batouti, may have been responsible for Batouti's irrational behavior when flying as Egypt Air's flight 990's relief officer, a Boeing 767 that, on October 31, 1999, was forced by him into the Atlantic Ocean about 60 miles south of Nantucket, Massachusetts. Joe briefs him and lends him his original USAF helmet and a life jacket for the flight. They are to fly VFR, and their ceiling will be restricted to the Class A, 18,000 ft floor. Giora climbs into the cockpit and studies.

Last minute briefing, its interior, before Joe is set to start the engine. Most of the instruments are westernized, but some are still the former Soviet design. The cockpit is small, and the instruments are all over the place with no logical order. He buckles up and locks the seatbelts and parachutes, connects the oxygen hose, and plugs in the communication cord. In an emergency, the ejection of both seats gets activated by either one of the pilots. Visibility from the back seat is quite restricted, and to help see forward, there is a periscope that gets deployed at taxiing, takeoff, and landing. They start the engine, call the tower for permission, and taxi to runway 27. Engine to 100%, afterburner deployed, and the craft rolls out at an accelerating rate. At 140 knots, they bring the nose up, and at 170, they rotate and take off.

| Taxing out | Taking off |

Dave and I get into Joe's flying buddy Dennis's L-29 and take off immediately following the MiG. The plan is to meet somewhere in the sky.

The MiG circles east towards the ocean, where we can maneuver the aircraft with few restrictions. In, literally, a fraction of a minute, the MiG is at 17,500 ft, and out of sight, Dave and I are trailing behind at a much lower rate of climb.

We could not find them without the help of a radar-equipped controller to vector us to the interception. We decided not to press too hard and upset some FAA regulators. We went on our own for fun in the blue sky. We landed a few minutes before the MiG to witness their arrival and Giora's impression of the encounter. Forty minutes after their departure, the 21 appear on final lands and taxis back to the hangar and towards us. Even looks dazed. He slowly climbs down and stops to look back, visibly shaken. "It's not so much of the flight or the MiG's performance that mesmerized me; the occasion of closing the circle is what threw meaway," he says.

He later commented that he preferred the French Mirage and the Nesher, in which he made history.

Back on Final

Another Saturday Morning Fun

CHAPTER FOUR
FLYING ACROSS AMERICA

n 2007, I acquired N300ME, a Mooney Ovation 3, made to my specs by the Mooney factory. I owned the now approx .. 1,300 hours Mooney for some fifteen years, taking me the 1,100 NM hop to Florida and

1,100 NM back almost every year, as well as to many other destinations. I think it's time to make the 5,500 NM trip to Los Angeles and back down to Boca Raton, visiting all the interesting sites America can offer on the way. So comes September, and the plan is made. The narrative below is taken from my blog and posted (more or less) daily.

So, weather (WX) permitting, on Sunday, Victor and I are going on an adventure across America. We'll be leaving Caldwell, NJ (CDW) eady, as planned, directly to Indianapolis (TYQ) and then to Omaha, NB (OMA). Should we not feel like continuing west on the same day, we'll go to Campaign, IL, some 93 NM north, to visit my friend Yoram and his wife Carole and stay the night. Here is the rest of the contemplated journey west:

October 2, OMA to Denver (DEN) and DEN to Yellowstone (COD)- will take a day for hiking.'

October 4, COD to Salt Lake City {SLC) and continuing to Reno, NV (RNO).

October 5, RNO to Sacramento, CA (MCC) and from there to Santa Monica, CA (SNO).

We'll be taking lots of pictures, especially over the Rockies and over the Sierra Mountains.After three days in LA, we'll start our way East-Itinerary to follow.

I have not posted anything since we left New Jersey on Sunday. Flying for 5 to 7 hours a day is simply exhausting. And the originally planned route is in the trashcan.

First, we discovered that the weather (WX) past Indianapolis through the Rockies was predictably bad for at least a week. While my friends Yoram and Carole invited us to stay with them, they would have had to suffer our presence for at least a week-so I changed the route and plotted a trip going to Louisville, KY (LOU)-581 NM, 3:16 hours, Tulsa, OK (TUL)-

512 NM, 3: 10 h, Santa Fe, NM (SAF) to Flagstaff, AZ (FLG) (Sedona and Grand Canyon)-512 NM, 3:26 h-and this is where we are today and tomorrow. Then we shall continue to Las Vegas (HND)-159 NM, 1:06 h, stay for a day or two and continue to Santa Monica, CA-240 NM, 1:31 h. Concluding some 2004 miles east to the west. We left NJ (CDW) on Sunday at 08:30 AM to LOU. All the way was uneventful over the eastern USA flatland. From LOU, we continued to Tulsa, OK (TUL), arriving at TUL sometimes after 4:00 PM local time. We flew both two legs in a day at 10,000 ft.

Victor was a perfect companion and partner. He had the capacity to share in an expensive trip, had exquisite taste in food and lifestyle, and had an expensive cigar aficionado. Victor was not a pilot but loved adventures. Before we reached any destination, he would call his secretary and ask her to research the best hotel and best restaurant in town, plus things to do in the area. Neither of us was pressed for time, so we were open to anything.

From TUL, we continued to Santa Fe (SAF) at 14000 ft. A beautiful city in an amazing setting. At the airport, I met Larry Salganek, the owner of Jet Warbirds, with whom I flew his MiG-15, T-33, L-29, L-39, and Fouga Magister, some 14 years earlier.

We rented a car and went to the famous Ojo Caliente mineral springs and spa, some 50 miles north of Santa Fe.

The flight from TUL to SAF was, for the most part, at 12,000 ft. in headwinds ranging from 37 to 47MPH. At some spots over high terrain, turbulence was quite severe. At the last pass over high terrain, we lost almost 3,000 ft. in a few seconds as the downdraft was overwhelming. Being a gliderpilot flying gliders over the Sierra Mountains, I knew to enter at a 45-degree angle, so we didn't have to confront sinking into the terrain. The landing was uneventful, with a high headwind.

OJO CALIENTE

This is a spa that was founded by the local Native Americans-there are 7 pools of different minerals to soak in, after which they wrap you in wool blankets for 30 min. Another experience. We then drove back to Santa Fe and booked a room at La Fonda hotel.

La Fonda Hotel is a traditional local hotel. Pleasant, but I wouldn't rate it too high. Santa Fe, however, is as beautiful as ever. In the evening, after returning from Ojo Caliente, we dined at The Bull Ring, an outstanding steak house. We enjoyed the Chateaubriand and the exquisite wine we were offered.

The following morning, we took off at around 09:00, heading "direct" to Flagstaff, AZ, elevation 7100 (FLG). The wind at takeoff was over 20 MPH, typical for the mountains. The headwind picked up as we climbed to 12,000 ft. and stayed all the way at a velocity of approximately 35 MPH. It took us some thirty minutes to climb a mere 5,000 ft. However, this time we confronted much wind shear. The wind shear was particularly disturbing on the final approach to FLG through landing. We were in a constant fight with the changes in altitude and stalled warnings throughout the approach and landing-a scary experience for a flatland pilot, yet the norm for the locals.

We rented a car and drove in scenic, stunning views of Sedona. A beautiful city with many top notch restaurants. We ate at Cucina Rustica. Another outstanding steak house, recommended by the owners of our 12-room rustic B & B. At the restaurant, we met Lisa Dahl, the owner of the restaurant, plus three others in town. Lisa invited us to join her at her Italian restaurant, Dahl & Deluca. Another superb restaurant.

In the morning, we drove to the Grand Canyon National Park, some 130 miles north of Sedona. There is nothing to add to this magnificent 8th Natural Wonders of The World. You've got to see it and be in awe.

Today we're going to fly our 5th leg west, the 5th day on the move. We'll be flying from FLG to Las Vegas, Henderson Airport (HND). We are cleared to 15,000 ft. to clear the surrounding mountains. The short 254-mile flight, 1:15 h to HND, is over stunning views of the Grand Canyon and the towering mountains around and then the Hoover Dam in the valley. I'm beginning to get used to the high-shifting winds, which are, as already mentioned, a daily routine for the local pilots in this part of the country.

Las Vegas is as vibrant as ever, nice for a day or two. Yet, still unique and worth visiting. We arrived early on Thursday, staying at the beautiful Wynn hotel. Victor and I had the greatest (and the most expensive ever) meal at the Wolfgang Puck restaurant at the MGM. The food was good for kings to enjoy, and the variety was stunning and so unusual. Later we enjoyed a great cigar at the Wynn. Such an opulent evening ...

We departed Las Vegas on Friday. The departure did not turn out ideal-we taxied to runway 21, awaiting Air Traffic Controller (ATC) to clear us. It was a wait of over 30 minutes in 95-plus degrees of heat with yet unknown departure time due to heavy traffic to Los Angeles. The wait resulted in the engine overheating, which forced us back to the ramp. We cooled the engine for another half hour while the tower's controller suggested we should depart via Visual Flight Rules (VFR) and then pick up our Instrument Flight Rules (IFR) plan in the air. Regardless, restarting the engine was not a piece of cake, and being concerned with draining batteries prompted us to order a booster (outside generator) to help start the engine without using battery power. We started the engine successfully, but one of the batteries was compfetely drained out.

At 11:30, we took off VFR. The flight took approximately 1:15 h to Santa Monica airport (SMO) in Los Angeles. We flew at 12,500 ft., passing the Sierra Mountains with just a little altitude to spare. Regardless, arriving at the Los Angeles Class B air space, I understood why our IFR release was delayed. Although New York air space is like a mad house, LA's were terribly congested and challenging. We found SMO and landed uneventfully. The next surprise came after landing; you see, the city of Santa Monica, with the support of the State of California and neighborhood residents, demanded to close the airport against all wishes of the General Aviation (GA) industry, including the FAA. Because of this, perhaps service businesses are not abundant, fearing the risk of closure. Regardless, and besides politics, there were very few services at the airport. We were instructed to park the plane at quite a distance and had to haul our luggage all that way to the airport exit.

Los Angeles was fun too. Although I don't appreciate its "charm," we managed to enjoy great food in some of the city's top restaurants. On the first night, we ate at a superb Japanese restaurant. I can clearly attest that this was the best Japanese food experience I have ever had. Afterthe meal, we went for a drink (and cigar) at a famous LA bar. There we met Gamal, the grandsonof Gamal Abdul Nasser, the late Egyptian leader during the Six-Day War. Nice guy, all the same!

So, Victor and Michael survived each other, in closequarters, throughout the entire journey from coast to coast!!!

In all truth, Victor turned out to be a great partner (not a pilot but a great company) in this adventure.

On Monday, October 9 (after restoring the dead battery and our own energy), I thought we should start the journey back to the east coast. Together, we agreed on the following itinerary:

Monday: LA (SMO) to Sacramento, CA (MCC) to Reno, NV (RNO), followed by stops in Salt Lake City (SLC), UT, Cody (COD), WY (Yellowstone Park), Denver (DEN), CO, Omaha (OMA), NB, Indianapolis (TYQ), ID and finally Caldwell (CDW), New Jersey, however, Victor had planned to see his family who was returning on Monday to LA from vacation, rather than making the trip back to the east coast-naturally, he gave other reasons. As I already stated, Victor is not a pilot, so his absence should not impact the flight back, yet we would miss some fun. I had no desire to go to some of the destinations alone, so I changed the returning itinerary. For now, the battery fault turned out to be a nonissue.

Monday: L. A. to Salt Lake City. Tuesday: SLC to Denver and DEN to Des Moines, Iowa (DSM). Wednesday: DSM to Champaign, IL, to visit my friends Yoram and Carole. Thursday: CMI to NJ.

Today (Monday), I went 540 miles to SLC alone. The wind was sometimes heading (32-37 MPH) and sometimes tailing (9 to 20 MPH). Amazing views of Las Vegas, the Grand Canyon, Hoover Dam, towering mountains up to 14,000 Ft, and Salt Lake. Traffic to the airport was quite busy, landing within a minut,e of one another. Salt Lake City is quite beautiful, set on the foot of some awesome mountains. I was invited by Karen and Steve, her Husband, for a lovely dinner at alocal upscale restaurant.

Before leaving for my next leg, the plane required maintenance and new parts to replace and repair. The mechanic at the local Fixed Base Operator (FBO) responsible was not to be available for another week, and then he would need to order parts from Texas and take some days to do the job, which would also bring the next annual inspection close. I didn't fancy staying in SLC for two weeks (or more) and then continuing the trip back home alone. I got a ticket on Delta and returned home. When ready, I shall go back and bring the plane home. Disappointing, to say the least. But I can't complain. Thus far, I have had a blast.

I booked a hotel and stayed the night in Salt Lake City. I then took the flight to Newark the following day.

So, as I said, Victor and I completed the trip going west across America. The adventure was amazing.

As mentioned, on the way back (alone), the plane had maintenance issues, and I could not afford the wait for the parts and repair. The plane was now ready for me to pick up, so I'm told, and I finished everything that was waiting to be done back in the office.

So, Lorraine, Hanan's my good friend's partner, offered to join me as a co-pilot on the trip from Salt Lake City to Boca Raton, Florida. We're scheduled to leave SLC on December 18, and I shall update the blog as we go along.

The route is planned, weather permitting, as follows:

Salt Lake City (SLC) to Denver, CO (DEN), 339 NM, DEN to Oklahoma City (OKC), 439 NM, OKC to Memphis (MEM), 375 NM, MEM to Tallahassee FL (TLH) 419 NM, TLH to Boca Raton, FL {BCT), 347 NM.

Altogether, 1919 NM calculated as approx. 11.1 flight hours (no wind).

We arrived in Salt Lake City to pick up the plane on Sunday, December 18. To our amazement, we were told that the annual inspection order would not be ready before Wednesday. We decided to tour Salt Lake City and its surroundings in the ensuing days-we found it to be well! worthwhile, so we went to visit the Mormon Temple in the city.

The temple square encompasses several buildings surrounding the temple itself (into whichonly Mormons are allowed}. The square is in themiddle of town and is very impressive in its beauty and grandeur. Mormon Volunteers from around the world attend it faithfully. The temple was built in the 18th century fromlocal granite mined from the surrounding canyons, all manually. It took 40 years to complete. In the following days, we visited Great Salt Lake State Park, including the Great Salt Lake and Bingham Canyon Copper mine, and Hills USAF Museum.

SALT LAKE

The lake contains about 26% salt, second only to the Dead Sea with 33%, yet there is life in the form of tiny shrimps in it. Millions of birds visit the lake each year to enjoy the abundant feast.

The Bingham Copper Mine

The Bingham Copper mine is considered the world's most productive copper mine. In recent years, it produced over 17 million tons of refined (99%) Copper, some 700 tons of pure Gold, some 6,000 tons of Silver, and many other minerals.

The Hill's Air Museum

The museum, one of many USAF museum venues, is dedicated primarily to local aviators and USAF veterans. All in all, an interesting museum exhibiting dozens of aircraft from WWII to (almost) the present day. On exhibit is a r,eplica of the Wright Brothers' first plane, B-52, B-29, C-130, 8-25, F-84, MiG-17, MiG-21, F-105, F-4, F-5, F-15, F-16, and countless more.

On Wednesday, we visited my plane in preparation for the following day's test flight plus the 470- mile flight to Santa Fe, replacing the planned flight to Denver due to bad weather at DEN. On Thursday, I made the short test flight which revealed nothing unusual.

We took off at 10:00 AM. The plane was heavy with all the bags and the 105 gallons of fuel we carried on board. So, the takeoff at the SLC 4,300-Ft elevation and our maximum weight were shallow and slow until we picked up speed.

As expected, the wind at 15,000 Ft was brutal. We confronted up to 70 knots of crosswind, mountain waves, and severe icing. I had to fly the plane manually most of the time due to continuous and rapid wind shear and removal of ice (I do have TKS certified for known icing)-1 used two gallons of the stuff. Turbulence was, at times, quite severe but otherwise tolerable. The view over the mountains was breathtaking. Due to cross and headwinds, it took some three and three-quarter-hour as opposed to the 2:54 planned. We used an amazingly low fuel flow of some 13GPH.

A problem emerged during the flight; apparently, the repair shop in SLC either didn't or erred in balancing and synchronizing the two ailerons, and I had to use hard rudder deflection to the left to keep the plane going straight. Regardless, we landed safely at SAF (elevation 6,400) and preparing for our flight to Oklahoma City (OKC) tomorrow. Now, the weather does not look promising beyond OKC either, but we shall see what tomorrow's forecasts reveal.

The forecast for the leg to Memphis and then Tallahassee was bad, so we plotted a new route going to Baton Rouge, LA (BTR), some 454 miles, approx. 3:00 h southeast and continuing to Tallahassee (TLH), FL, another 360 miles further east. The weather to BTR was solid IFR (Instrument Flight Rules) all the way, with much icing, thick clouds, and strong cross andtailwinds.

On the final approach, my windshield was covered with opaque ice-not fun. I used theside widow and Synthetic Vision (SV) to see and aim at the runway. Landed safely, fueled, and took off toward TLH. Here again, confronted with solid IFR and bad weather. With no special issues, we landed in TLH in the afternoon. Greeted with a warm 70-degree (F°) temp after freezing weather of+\- 22° F (minus 5.6° C) in the prior three cities.

On Sunday, December 24, at approx. 10:00, we took off into a low ceiling, which improved rapidly and warmed further as we went south. Arrived in Boca around noon time.

So, the entire trip took about 5,149 NM (approx. 9,345 KM) in 31.5 flight hours. To sum it up, this was a trip of a lifetime. America is beautiful, with breathtaking views, venues, places of immense interest, and friendly people everywhere. It is al1so enormous.

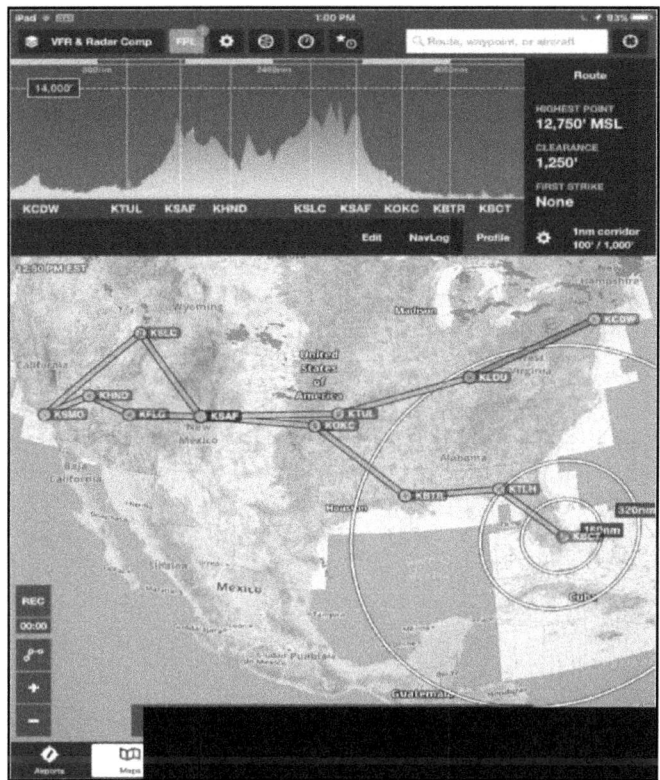

Above is a map with the routes of the entire trip:

WESTBOUND

Caldwell, NJ (CDW). Louisville, KY (LOU). Tulsa, OK (TUL). Santa Fe, NM (SAF), Flagstaff, AZ (FLG), Las Vegas, NV (HND), and Santa Monica, CA (SMO).

EASTBOUND

Santa Monica, CA (SMO), Salt Lake City, UT (SLC), Santa Fe, NM (SAF), Oklahoma City, OK (OKC), Baton Rouge, LA (BTR), Tallahassee, FL (TLH), Boca Raton, FL (BCT).

CHAPTER FIVE
FLYING AFRICA SAFARI

"Why is it you can never hope to describe the emotions Africa creates? You are filled. Out of whatever pit, unbound from whatever tie, released from whatever fear. You are lifted, and you see it all from above."

Francesca Marciano- Rules of the Wild

I was sitting in my office one Spring Day, engulfed with the doldrum of the mundane life of the city. Fed-up with the bombardments of endless mind-boggling political messages, I am thinking of an easy exit into *something else* which may elevate my mood. A blip from my computer calls my attention to a new message in my email Inbox. I open it and find a notification announcing the gathering of a group of pilots (and some passengers) to participate in a flying safari tour in Africa. Wow, is that what I needed ... ?

Craig is an operator of a South African Bush Flying school. "A very experienced pilot and extremely friendly," I'm told by Alon, who helps Craig gather pilots to join the several tours each year and who introduced me to the project. Craig is also trained in guiding tours and is loaded with historical information on Africa, its people, and wildlife. For his tours, he attracts pilots and nonpilots to join. Pilots, who would fly the LSA aircraft, would need to demonstrate some experienceflying and are supposed to train at Craig's field (dubbed "Eve's Field") to show competency.

Savanna S ICP   Savage Cub, Bobber

The participating pilots are also required to pass a State flying test and obtain a South African license. Four planes participate in each tour, two Savannas and two Savage Cubs. Two-sitter Ultralights, the Savage, also called "Bobber," is a tail dragger while the Savannahs are nose wheel try-cycles.

Savannah S*		Savage Bobber*
Manufactured:	Piedmont, Italy	Czech Republic
Wingspan:	29 Ft	21 Ft
Powerplant:	Jabiru 2200 (80 HP) replaced by	Rotex 912 UlS (l00HP)
Wing Area:	138.5 Sq. Ft	153. Sq. Ft.
Empty Weight:	631 lb.	635 lb.
Gross Weight:	992 lb.	1,235 lb.
Fuel Capacity:	20.6 gall.	17 gal.
Cruise Speed:	111 mph	110mph
Stall Speed:	30mph	39 mph
	*As published by the manufacturer	

" ... One cannot resist the lure of Africa."

Rudyard Kipling

I was always intrigued by what I read about Africa. Yet, while a trip there was certainly on my *bucket list* until now, I haven't prioritized it. A few years ago, a gliding buddy revealed to me the outstanding gliding conditions in Namibia, situated just west of Botswana and northwest of South Africa's northern border. A group of them, I was told, are going there every few years--1 almost enlisted. He never told me about the people and the continent; this I acquired from some of the many enticing kinds of literature written about Africa. This time, I was determined not to miss this unique opportunity to engage my emotions with this mystical land. Bush Flying there would, of course, be a bonus.

Vachellia tortilis. Widely known as Acacia tortilis but now attributed tothe genus Vachellia, is the umbrella Thom acacia, also known as umbrella thorn and Israeli baboon, a medium to large, canopied tree native primarily to the six million years of the savannas, and Sahel of Africa.

"The only man I envy is the man who has not yet been to Africa-for he has so much to look forward to."   Richard Mullin -- Explorer

So, I'm booked. Sent all the required documents and am ready to go. Last night, quoting my mother'spopular saying, "I didn't sleep a wink." And I doubt my journey from JFK to JNB (16 hours in coach)and then to PIETERMARITZBURG (PZB) would offer any further relief. I'm, naturally, apprehensive about my ability to fly in a straight line the following day when arriving at Eve's Field for training. Yet, I'm still excited about the adventure I'm about to experience.

Waiting for me at PZB's gate are Craig and Nir, and we drive to Eve's Field to meet the rest of the group.

Left to right; Nir, Maoz, and Roy

The group consists of five pilots; Maoz, Roy, Shmuel, Nir, and me, and two passengers; Tzila (Maoz's wife) and Haim (Shmuel's brother). We meet with a group of highly spirited people and the treatment by Craig, as I'm about to find, is royal from start to finish. The comradery was established immediately. While older than most by decades, to my dismay, I was treated by all as the elderly who deserve special respect (I got to sit in the front seat of the van, and Nir made sure to make my morning tea)-sweet people, none-the-less. Roy oversaw making coffee throughout the trip.

Craig, Haim, Shmuel and Zila

For accommodations during our local stay, we were provided with a room each in a guesthouse up the hill, belonging to Craig's brother and managed by Sam, Craig's wife. It is a typical colonial house with all the charm and conveniences. Victor, the housekeeper, roams around to ensure everyone's approval. "We'll come to pick you up for breakfast and then train at 07:00 AM," Craig announces.

Nir makes sure to make me the morning tea... what a pal.

Breakfast at a local cafe (just off Main Street).

Training and Foreign License Validation

"We are going to fly to a nearby airstrip and practice flying the Savanna and the Bobber. "There would only be two aircraft flying at the time. The rest of you should work on the SA written test. In between, just hang around the hangar and wait your turn." This is when we officially form Eve's Parliament. Thewritten test covers almost identical topics to the US ones, only that if the last time you did it was over forty years ago, it would take *some help* recalling. Regardless, "no captive's left behind," and we all pass with high scores. "Out there, we would fly in a formation of four."

We all rush to fuel and prepare the planes for our First flight.

Eve Field's Parliament in session

The training phase is completed, and the formal Foreign License Validation certificates are received just in time for commencing the first leg of our Safari trip. We are invited tonight to a BBQ dinner at Craig's house. Sam, a lovely and beautiful lady (about a hundred years younger than I), and their beautiful little girl are hosting us. Lang's home was beautiful and very inviting.

We enjoyed some delicious South African dishes, including the local equivalent of American Grits and the equivalent, yet more appealing, version of the American Beef-Jerky. Of course, there were steaks and sausages, as a decent BBQ would command.

We are to be picked up for briefing at 7:00 AM the following morning.

First Leg: Eve's Field to FAHL (Hluhluwe) - FAAM (Amsterdam Mpumalanga)- FALL (Lydenburg Maplandia)

In the briefing, we are told that we are to fly to our first fuel stop at Hluhluwe (FAHL, 249 MSL), a strip some 113 NM northeast of Durban (DUR). We are to fly at 150 to 200 ft. AGL along the shoreline and some flatland until later, we get to the highland following Amsterdam Mpumalanga. From FAHL, we shall continue to Amsterdam Mpumalanga (FAAM, 4310 MSL) and finally to Lydenburg Maplandia (FALL, 4880 MSL). The total flight distance for the day is estimated at approx. 323 NM in about 4.1 hours. Craig's Savage Cub is leading our formation, with two Savannas at Nos. 2 and 3 positions and the other Bebber (Savage Cub), flown by Maoz and Tzila to follow as the formation's no. 4. Haim is to fly with his brother Shmuel and Nir and me to rotate between the two Savannahs. There are no wildlife sightings expected along this route until we reach the game reserve the following day. The scenery, however, is stunning all along the way. We are on our way at about 08:00 AM.

Years ago, when I first learned how to fly the Piper Cub, I was told by my instructor to constantly look for a possible emergency landing site. These days that was switched to a search for the next spot to relieve ourselves ...

After about two hours of butt-aching flight, we arrive at the shoreline. We flew, almost touching the waves .

Overwhelmed with the amazing landscape, we finally arrive at our first refueling destination (FAHL) and land safely to relieve the aircraft's thirst and our aching butts.

"Nothing but breathing the air of Africa, and actually walking through it, can communicate the indescribable sensation ... "

William Burchell - English Explorer

Indeed, God granted Africa a huge share of the planet's beauty, and pictures speak a thousand words.

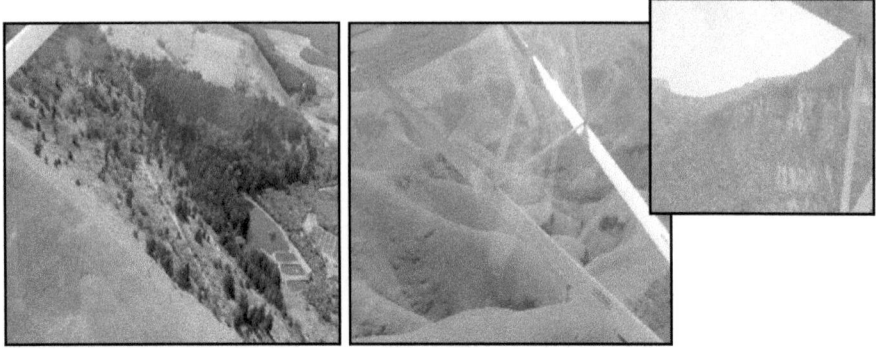

Fllying further to the northwest got us to Amsterdam Mpumalanga (FAAM), which, while designated "airport," is nothing resembling what we experienced a facility of the same description to be. Yet, amazingly, the beauty of the desolated land can neither be compared to anything we experienced; the deep silence, endless visibility, and sense of belonging are inimitable.

One more short leg takes us to Lydenburg Maplandia (FALL). While at FAAM, we 1level the fuel supply from each other's fuel tanks, at FALL, there is ample supply waiting for us.

Next, we'll be going to our final stop of the day and our first Game Lodge-Honeyguide Tented Safari Camp at the Manyeleti Game Reserve in Kruger National Park.

The controlilers must have forgotten to show up to work...

So, we landed on the strip and parked next to the driver, who was already waiting to pick us up.

We shall bestaying at the lodge for two nights and taking three

Safari trips over the next two days. Anderson (I think) is our driver-he would be sitting on the front bonnet of the "Jeep" (actually, Toyota) to guide and spot interesting wildlife in sight on our safari trips. There would be two safaris on the first day, leaving at 06:00 AM, returning at about 09:00 AM, and one at 16:00 and returning just after dusk.

At the lodge, we are assigned cabins and offered drinks upon arrival. Dinner to follow on a reserved table set up for us in advance.

We're advised not to walk alone at night, and Anderson (I think) escorts us with his flashlight between the cabins and the dining area. Sure, enough, an elephant bull approached, too close for comfort, but Anderson skillfully chased him away.

As already customary to this group, the jokes flow non-stop around the dinner table. Maoz is the invincible king of jokes! So, here is a joke I forgot to tell:

What makes the mind of a pilot?

An old lady married to an old pilot was praying to God every day. Pleading wishes from the all-mighty.

One morning, she opened her prayer with a new request; "God," she said, "as you know., I was a dedicated Christian all/my life. I Helped the poor, donated to charity., and prayedevery single day. As you also know., I hate flying., yet I always yearned to see Hawaii before I die. Can you please build a highway between Los Angeles and Hawaii? I'm stilla good driver, and I can drive the highway to Hawaii without a problem."

She suddenly hears a voice coming from above:

Lady, the deep voice said, a highway over a long and deep ocean is engineeringly almost impossible. Why don't you pick an easier wish for me to fulfill?

Oh, said the lady, then how about explaining to me ... what makes the mind of a pilot?

There was silence for a few seconds. Then the voice came in again:

"... how many lanes would you like on that highway?"

Drums, please ...

At 06:00, we begin our first safari trip. We chose our seats on the Jeep (actually Toyota), and greeting us was George, our wildlife guide. As we leave the camp, we witness the amazing sunriseso typical of Africa.

If I have ever seen magic, it has been in Africa

Jack Hemingway-writer, son of Ernest

The Manyeleti Game Reserve is adjacent to the open-border Kruger National Park and adjacent to the Sabi Sand Private Game Reserve, as well as the Timbavati Game Reserve. The Tsonga people, who occupied the land before colonization, were forcefullly removed and displaced from this land by the colonizers. In the local language, Manyeleti means 'place of the stars.' Its 23,000 hectares of savanna are home to the Big Five mammals, many more predators, herbivores, and over 300 species of bird. We were lucky to see wildlife in their natural habitat, inclusive of predators and their prey.

Vultures, giraffes, and elephants

A leopard safeguarding her prey on a nearby tree

Hyenas awaiting leftovers beneath the leopard's tree

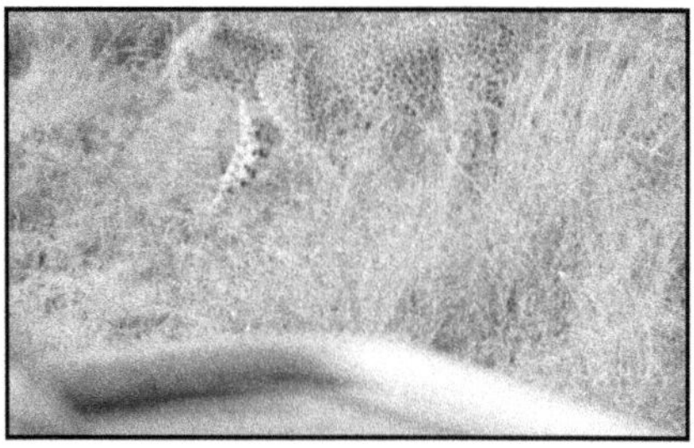

At 09:00, we are back in the camp for breakfast. We have until 16:00 to rest and kill time. Some chose to take a massage, as I did-I found the quality of the massage to be below average. The afternoons are incredibly quiet as the temperatures rise, and all living creatures look for shelter from the sun's scorching rays.

The night safari is a lookout for predators out to catch a meal. An hour before dusk, George suggests a walk back to the camp. Walking through the savanna, we see a skeleton of a hippopotamus killed by poachers. The skeleton is purposely left on the ground for all to see.

Then, he spots a pile of Impala's droppings and instructs us to pick, two dropping balls each, claiming there is nothing contaminating in his mouth, and blows as eject them. He places two hard as he can to each as far as he can.

"The winner will receive a title gift to be held throughout his stay at the camp" (Tzila and Maoz are not present during this evening safari). Reluctantly, we each took part in the contest-I still don't believe I did it! The winner was Haim, who shut the balls almost 10 ft. George crowns him with the title of "King of Shit" for the duration.

At sundown, we return to the camp.

This morning we are taking another safari at 06:00 and then heading to the "airport" to commence the second leg of the trip. We say goodbye to the camp's staff.

Getting ready to go the long ride to Madikwe Game Reserve. We pack breakfast, and off we go.

Landing on a corn field

Madikwe Game Reserve is one of the largest reserves in South Africa, spanning 75,000 hectares of dry Bushveld. The area consists largely of thornveld on clay soil in the North and broad-leaved vegetation further south on dolomite soils. The landscape, although devoid of rivers, apart from the Marica River on the eastern boundary, is very striking, with large flat expanses interrupted by pointed hills referred to as the Enselbergs.

In 1991, the Madikwe area was established as a game park, and the mission and schooling made the headquarter of the Northwest Park Board. In 1992, the largest relocation of animals at the time was in the Southern Hemisphere (Operation Phoenix). It resulted in the introduction of over twenty-four large mammal species and over eight thousand heads of the game. For example, the relocation included the introduction of eleven lions, around two hundred elephants and 66 buffalos, 1200 zebra and 1000 Blue wildebeest, and some 2000 impalas. Today, the reserve boasts a strong lion population of over seventy, over five hundred elephants, and roughly 400 buffalo.

Roy, Nir, and Maoz at the pool (elephant watching)

Tau offers nice accommodations and easy access to the most amazing game park in Madikwe. We are staying at Tau for two nights before finally returning to Eve's Field.

Our wildlife guide is Mike (also likes to be called Ray), and we start the morning safari, as usual, at 06:00AM.

Mike is deeply knowledgeable; he has been acting as a guide for the past five years and has become an expert in all wildlife present in Madikwe via schooling and practice.

"You know you are truly alive when you're living among the lions .... "

Isak Dinesen-Out of Africa

The variety and intensity of animals in such a restricted area are overwhelming at Madilkwe. We searched and found the real Black Reino and even lions sharing hunted Impala.

Impalas and Boars in the wilds

Some have breakfast at the Park

Walking the Safari

So are we

So, at the safari hike, we get to our "Gin and Tonic" spot. Mike/Ray gets the drinks out, and we joke around. Up to this point, I considered myself young and fit. Now, this bunch is years younger than I, and while they do, I don't see it until this:

I climbed on a tree for a photo shot, but when I attempted to climb down, seven pairs of hands rushed to help me stay steady getting down ... this branch was some 5 ft AGL... now, that is embarrassing ...

Embarrassing moment

"If there were one more thing I could do, it would be to go on safari again."

Karen Blixen - Out of Africa

We participated in three safaris at Madikwe with much satisfaction, lots of fun, and much comradery. We shall soon continue to our last stop for the night at Zuikerkop.

Early take off with one stop for coffee and breakfast at Parys. Watched some paratroopers perform a free fall to a target near us. Reminds me of the five jumps I was required to do *many* years ago ...

Zuikerkop is a large farm (of some 30,000 hectares, I believe) and a nice Guest House owned by a well-to-do family working the land and other businesses. The manager meets us at the strip, used by the family to operate the variety of aircraft they own and store at an adjacent hangar. A Pilatus PC-12 lands moments after our arrival, and a son of the owner emerges to help us top our aircraft with fuel that Craig reserved for us.

At the lodge, we are first invited for drinks (and jokes) on a beautiful terrace overlooking a magnificent view. We then proceed to a nice dining room for our dinner. More jokes and laughs together with exquisite food and wine. Great evening.

We only have a couple of hours of flight to Eve's Field, and Craig decides we would have enough time to stop and visit Destiny Castle on our way without jeopardizing the departure time for Air Link to take us back home.

The castle, built by its eccentric owner, is completed but unoccupied. The short strip intimidates somehow, as it ends at the edge of the mountain.

It is all worth it. The castle is unique and in stark contrast to its surroundings. We walk a short distance to the castle and meet the caretakers who are permanently on the property.

We take off to our destination filled with thousands of moments to cherish for a lifetime. I slept 10 hours in my Business Class seat on the way home.

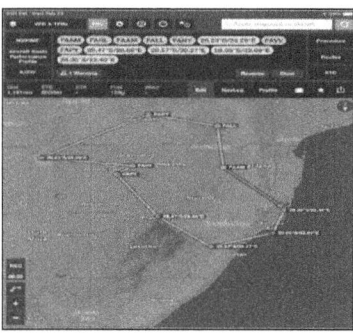

"I never knew a morning in Africa when I was not happy."

Ernest Hemingway

Unfortunately, a few months after our return home, Craig had a flying accident when exploring a new route for his flying guests. He collided with power lines and crashed in a remote location in South Africa. The accident robbed this great guy of his young life. RIP Craig.

CHAPTER SIX
FLYING LOW AND SLOW

My friend, Mookie, purchased a Lockwood AirCam kit, built it, and, together with other AirCam owners, flew it from Sebring, Florida (KSEF) to Billing, Montana (KBIL). Due to some extraneous circumstances and reasons, he left the aircraft in Billing until an opportunity arose to bring it back to New York, where it would stay for the season.

Mookie was a Mirage fighter in the Israel Airforce (IAF). He's a very competent pilot and a good friend.

A need arose back in 1995 for the National Geographic Society for a slow aircraft for photography in Africa where they had to fly low and slow to capture images, with no space to land. Phil Lockwood offered to build such a plane, and so he did.

The AirCam, equipped with two Rotax 912, 4-cycle engines generating some 100 HP each, became a perfect design. It flies as slow as 40 MPH (stalls at 39 MPH) and up to 100 MPH with a gross weight of 1,680 lbs. and a rate of climb of 1,500 Ft/Min-it takes off in less than a couple of hundred feet. The AirCam has great visibility, almost 300 degrees around, and amazing maneuverability while taxiing on the ground. The 36 ft.-

wingspan craft holds 28 gallons of either Avgasor auto gasoline. With a range of 240 miles at 80 to 90 MPH and 3:30-hour endurance, it burns impressively low 8.0 GPH or so. It seats two, and you can buy a canopy that shields both occupants from the wind buffer and other natural elements. Mookie added the canopy to his Purchase.

Lockwood AirCam N148BB

Since 1995, 160 AirCam Kits have been built and sold. **So, one morning, Mookie called and asked if I would mind joining him as a saf,ety pilot to bring his craft to New York. I agreed, and on the agreed date, we flew (commercially) to Billing, MN.**

Four Dances National Park

The following morning, we arrived at Billing Logan International Airport (BIL), where the AirCam was hangered. The plane was topped off with avgas and the appropriate oil additive. We stored our luggage in the quiet, roomy storage behind the backseat and got ready to go. I entered the back seat and got familiarized with the avionics and controls. The back cockpit is VFR equipped with the addition of an ADS-B monitor. As discussed, we planned to fly as low as practical to enjoy the view and unique topography. Mookie plotted the first-day, three-leg route, which would be taking us almost 600 miles eastward.

We took off at BIL, and I was amazed at this little aircraft's rate of climb-straight up at, I assume, some 8 to 12 degrees. The first leg was from Billing, MT (BIL) to Bowman, ND (BWW), going east. That took us over the Yellowstone River and the 765 acres of the undeveloped Four Dance National Park. 200 to 500 ft. cliffs mounted on the west side of the river. A beautiful sight of this winding river. We arrived at Bowman after approximately 2.5 h and 234 miles. Bowman County is a mix of hills and flatland awash with prevailing winds, which drive the dozens of electricity-generating windmills. We had fun flying between and below the windmills at 100 to 200 feet of altitude-I can assure you; I'd never attempt this stunt in my Mooney...

Lawrence and Custer Counties, SD

The next leg is from BWW to Black Hills Airport - Clyde Ice Field, Spearfish, SD (SPF), a short 103 NM. We took off going south to SPF with the idea was visiting Mount Rushmore, National Park. Spearfish Park and Spearfish Creek are mountainous and deep canyons recreational areas of the Spearfish Canyon in Lawrence County, SD. Believe it or not, the entire area was submerged by the sea some 600 years ago. When the water subsided 30 to 60 million years ago, masses of land began to appear, and the drainage formed the Spearfish Canyon, as well as other water ravines feeding it from all sides. Trees and plants from the Rocky Mountains, the eastern woodland, and the Great Plains areas can be found.

Lawrence and Custer Counties, SD, are popular tourist destinations. They include the famous gold-rush Deadwood city, Sylvan Lake, and Wildlife Loop Road.

At SPF, we met the two partners who run the local FBO (Fixed Base Operator), who was very helpful in advising us about visiting Mount Rushmore, only some 41 miles southeast. Unfortunately, the weather was not cooperative, and we decided to skip the site. We regret not waiting out the weather or driving to this important destination.

From SPF, we pushed on to Miles City, MT, at Frank Wiley Field (MLS), some 146 NM NW. We landed, refueled, and immediately started the long leg to Aberdeen, SD (ABR), some 316 NM east. We avoided the mountains and went along riverbanks and flatlands. Second-day flying took us some 799 NM in an easterly course. So, we ended up on the second day with long 9.7 hours over 799 miles low and slow. We stayed the night at Aberdeen in a hotel near the airport.

The plan for the second day is to do 430 miles from ABR to Mankato Regional, Mankato, MN

(MKT), a 206 NM lleg in 2.5 h. From MKT, we are planning to go to Platteville Airport, WI (PVB), a 178 NM, 2.6 h, and on the final leg, planned for a stop for the night at Albertus Freeport, IL (FEP), a mere 46 miles southeast. For most of the flight, all legs were in flatland with no significant sites except for many windmills all along the way. At the last minute, we decided to skip FEP and continue to Joliet, IL (OT), as we had plenty of daylight still ahead. This diversion added some 77 NM to a total of 1.5 h. We ended the day with 507 NM and 6.6 h of flight. Lots of wind, much flatland, and bountiful greenery all around.

The third day begins with a leg to Kendallville, IN (C62}, 131 NM East, and from there to Willoughby Lost Nation (LNN), another 174 NM east, and a stop for the day. We flew about a mile into Lake Erie at 100 ft over the water and along the shore until just before Erie International/ Tom Ridge Field (KERI), PA. The flight over the water and along the shore was magnificent, but we had to turn inland to avoid the air space and direct to LNN for the night. We accomplished the target and spent some 5.1 h covering 305 NM of an exciting cross-country flight, slow and low.

At 100 IFt, upon Lake Erie along its southern shoreline

Tomorrow's going to be our fourth and last day before we reach Sky Acres, New York (44N). There would be two legs totaling 350 NM from LNN to our destination.

So, we got up early in the morning, and soon after breakfast, we fueled and went on our way to Wellsboro Johnson Airport, Wellsboro, PA (N38). The area is already very familiar to us, Northeast pilots. We land at N38, a nice little airport with nice people running the FBO. There are a few warbirds in the field, and its pastoral surrounding is calming and captivating. We load with coffee and fuel and take off straight east to Sky Acres. To be sure, the hills and mountains are becoming more and more familiar as we get closer to the Catskills and upstate New York. We arrive some 6.8 hours after our morning departure and store the plane at the hangar space Mookie reserved.

While the flight across the country was elating, the commute back to New Jersey was not something to cherish. But that is for another story.

I had a great time with Mookie and his new toy. Next, I shall see him at our next $100 hamburger or the $250 lobster gathering.

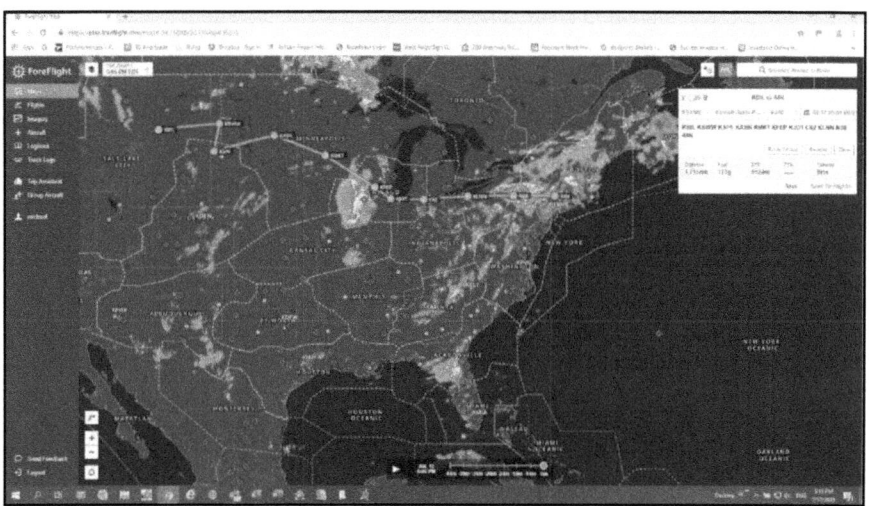

Billing MT to Sky Acres, NY, the entire route

CHAPTER SEVEN
FLYING; THE ALPS

I've been flying gliders for some fifteen years. I bought my first glider, DG-303 Elan N042ME, almost soon after I began soaring. The DG-303 Elan has a 15-meter wingspan with a glide ratio of approximately 40 to one. I flew it for about six years in many venues in the USA, mainly in contests, and in our own home field, N82, in Wurtsboro, NY. I'm not an outstanding glider-pilot but a pretty good one, but via this amazing sport, I got to know world soaring champions such as George Moffat, Karl Striedieck, Steve Fossett, Tom Knauf, and many others.

One of my flying buddies at the airport was Bob Leve, a professor at Hartford University and an avid aviator. Together, Bob and attended several gliding contests and always had a blast. In one contest, I had to retrieve him when he landed out in a cornfield some 180 miles away from the starting base-the retrieve was an all-night affair, there and back.

My Nl50ME DG-303 Elan in Wurtsboro, New York (N82)

One Saturday afternoon, I received a call from Bob. It was a winter day, cold and miserable. Bob was telling me of his experience of a whole week of flying in the French Alps. He then proceeded to ask if I would want to join him that coming March to fly the French Alps in France's Southeastern commune of Saint-Auban. I immediately agreed, and we began coordinating the details.

On a swiveling drive of Alpes Maritimes

Saint-Auban, population 300, is an ancient village at the foot of the huge Tragastel Rock in the Alpes Maritimes and Cote Azur, an hour drive from the French Riviera. From New York, you take a (commercial) flight to Nice and rent a car to go up the magnificent whirling drive to Saint-Auban. In March, as planned, I depart for Nice and meet Bob the following day. Bob rented a car, and off we went on the swirling narrow road that takes us up the mountains, with too many scary curves. They call them "balcony roads." Regardless, Bob is driving like a maniac up the road.

Our destination: Centre National De Vol a Voile aerodrome (www.cnvv. net), a State-run soaring club. The club is equipped with some 25 state-of-the-art sailplanes for every class and a crew of gliding-expert instructors. We finally find the aerodrome and head to the office to present our registrations and credentials and to be assigned rooms in the cabins. "You start training tomorrow at 08:00, immediately after breakfast-lunch at 12:00," we were told. Of the seven days we are supposed to fly the mountains, two to three would be with instructors. Thereafter, we're on our own. We were given sketchy maps (hand-drawn) showing the probable lift in the area as well as guiding us in the maze in which these mountains are arranged.

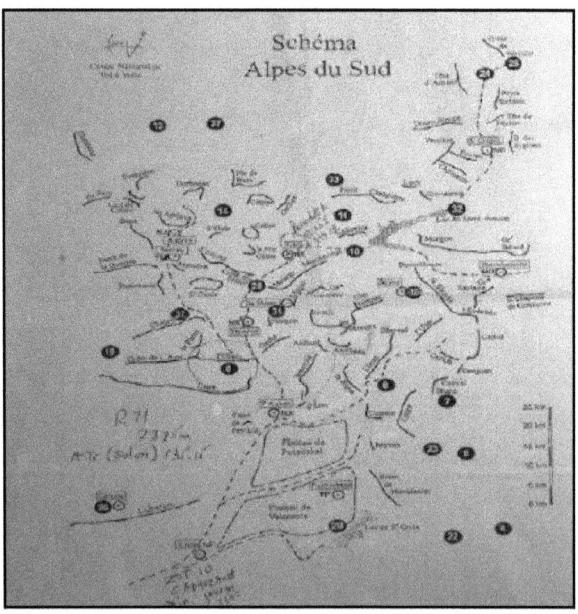

We were given a schematic map of probable lift and passage locations

Now, research would reveal that in a period of ten years, sailplanes in the Alps endured 225-250 accidents with 92 -100 fatalities. Most accidents occur by French pilots, and most by flying into terrain. In retrospect, I can personally attest to the French's daredevil flying. "Do we get GPS instruments?" I ask. "You will not need one," the answer was. Only later, I'll understand what they meant. As for air collisions, Europe largely solved that problem for gliders by introducing the FLARM, a traffic awareness avoidance system. It is similar, in concept, to ADS-B, though simpler and much cheaper, while very effective. Europe used it for years successfully. FLARM is important simply because, in a busy thermal, there could be 20 or 30 gliders circling within inches from each other-the FLARM watches their back somewhat.

The Mountains everywhere I flew, and especially in the USA, are somehow arranged in ridges going Northwest to Southeast or Northeast to Southwest, including the Rockies. Not the Alps! The 4,000 meters (+/-13,000 ft) Alps have no specific order. Some ridges go North-South, and others go East-West, merging into each other. That creates a problem for a sailplane flying the Alps. Many times, theridges create a V-shaped valley when they merge. So, when entering the formation, thinking of the "valley" supposedly going east towards the starting field (following GPS), you surprisingly discover that you have entered two (or more) merging towering mountains, creating a dead-end passage if you are below their 14,000 ft. peaks with little or impossible room to turn around. That never stopped the French instructors from maneuvering with over sixty-degree bank, inches from the rocks-thus, the accidents rate.

Mount Authon

You must study and know the area well to fly it on your own. That's the rule of surviving soaring the Alpes. Yet, as difficult as it may be to maneuver the Alps, the scenes are breathtaking. Whether you are high above the peaks or close to the rocks, it is awesome.

At 5,000 meters (15,000 ft), looking East towards St de Cheval Blanc

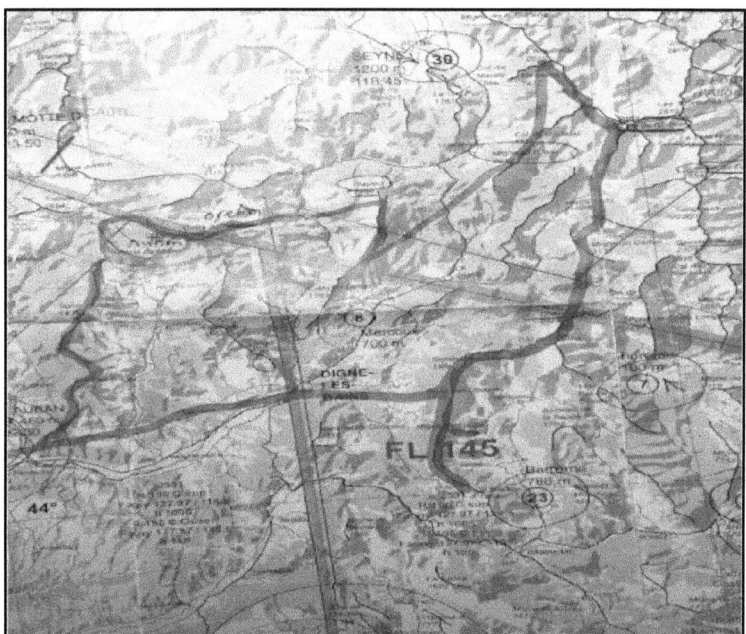

A real Map of the French Alpes marked with my task

On the third day, I take a task covering multiple summits (see map above). Pilon is the first ridge you pick when released from the tow plane. A relatively small mountain that enables you to jump onto the 4,800 ft. high Sammet de Vaumuse. This relatively long ridge (approx. 15 NM) provides for good ridge flying (le vol de pente) when the wind is 30 degrees or perpendicular to the ridge. It gets deflected by it, and a lift is created from the rising air.

Many pilots go back and forth on Vamoose to gain altitude to the next level or just for fun. The next move requires at least an additional 1,800 ft. to reach 1,000 ft above the 5,636 ft Authon's summit. Alternatively, embarrassed, you go back home. I did not embarrass myself. At the northwest side of this awesome rock of Authon, I circle and gain additional 1,500 ft needed to leap northeast to Blayeul, 2,200 m (7,300 ft) altitude. Blayeul is a beautiful mountain, and I see a few mountain bikers and climbers on a narrow path on top of the mountain. Cool! From Blayeul, I leap to Mtgne Rubac, which is a few hundred feet lower in altitude, to avoid Aiguillette, which is 2,000 ft taller, and proceed to Liman and cross the valley to Cheval Blanc, down Coupe to Coulson, and back to St Auban. The total flight time in the club's Duo Discus today is 3:00 hours. In six days, I flew about 12 hours. A wonderful experience, no doubt.

Happy Hour on the campus begins at 12:00 PM, lunchtime, at 14:00, they all are back in their gliders, "flying high!"

CHAPTER EIGHT
FLYING TO COMPETE

"If you hear a voice within you, saying 'you cannot paint,' then, by all means, paint, and that voice will be silenced.

Vincent Van Gogh

Soaring gliders, by itself, in my view, is the most challenging form of flying. Competing in this form is the ultimate test of your aviation skills. When I heard of the achievements of some of the champions in that sport, I was convinced I'd never come close.

Yet, at the beginning of my soaring days (with less than 50 hours in a glider), I managed to acquire the international soaring organization's (Federation Aeronautique lnternationale--FAI) Gold Badge for reaching at least 3,000 meters (9,842 ft) in altitude-I soared up to 18,000 ft; going for a distance of at least 300KM (186.4 SM)-I surpassed 250 miles, for a duration of at least 5 hours-I stayed up there longer. That boosted my confidence (ironicallly) to believe that I could now compete.

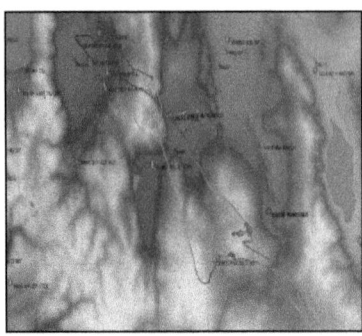

My 259.2 SM run in Nevada

Soaring contests are performed in many venues around the world, all sanctioned by FAI and all by the same rules. There are several different methods (tasks) to fly each time and rules governing each type. There are several organizations in the USA that are helpful to beginner contestants: The Sailplane Racing Association (SRA) and the Soaring Society of America (SSA). They both have a wealth of information concerning everything to do with soaring and soaring contests.

Naturally, the focus is on safety. As gliders get a lift from specific sources (thermals, mountain waves, ridge lift, etc.) at distinct locations, all contesting gliders get attracted to these sites. As a single contest may consist of 30 to 50 gliders, these sites can get very crowded. It is not unusual to see gaggles of twenty or more gliders circling in the same thermal, inches from each other- within an air cylinder no larger than two wingspans wide and a few hundred feet high. To avoid a collision, you must be aware of your situation and be razor-sharp and proficient in your flying, keeping it steady amongst the others in all dimensions-never-the-less, it is no less exhilarating.

Contestants are lining up for the initial tow to 2,000 feet

Many times, birds of all kinds, including buzzards and eagles, would join the dance.

Since contestants push their skills to the max, obviously, some may lose their ability to sustain flight and are forced to crash land in some field or remote airport. It is, therefore, a prerequisite demand of participants to show evidence of numerous "landing out" before they can participate-I landed out numerous times, at least six in contests.

A friend of mine landed some 180 miles from the starting base, and we spent the night retrieving him. I learned to love landing out, especially in a remote field or on a hilltop, absorbing the scent and sounds of nature.

A couple of landing Out in my DG 303

A contest may span over seven to fourteen days. A task is given each day and usually consists of three or more turning points to which contestant gliders should arrive. You are given a minimum duration and distance for the task, all of which are recorded on the glider's GPS device. At the end of the day, the pilots submit the GPS file to the judges to score the flight. The fastest flight over the flown distance gets the higher score. Usually, the daily task covers from one hundred to three hundred miles, or more, for the minimum set duration. My callsign was "Mike Echo - ME," and so were all my aircraft I owned marked.

Of course, there are specialty record flights that brought gliders up well into the stratosphere (2018 record 76,000 feet) and to a distance world record of 3,008 KM (approx. 1,823 SM, in 2003).

An early version of GPS recorder

So, each morning the gliders get assembled and lined up on the runway to be towed by multiple tow planes to 1,500-2,000 Ft. AGL, where they are released and climb to the Starting Gate altitude where each start begins.

Gliders in their trailers ready for assembly

In one of my early contests in Mifflin County, PA, I made the grave mistake of following George Moffatt (world champion) and Hank Nixon (U.S. Champion). Both climbed the thermal in minutes, leaving me struggling to retain my altitude at the base of that thermal-I wonder if they had a good laugh... So, I pushed the envelope so much with so few skills to match what was left, with no discerned options to remain in flight. The terrain below is very unfriendly. Rocky and hilly with no field insight. Yet, if dared landing, it is an ideal place for breaking a fiberglass glider into small pieces. I circle tight, looking for a glimpse of a thermal that I can hang on to. No luck. I'm losing altitude rapidly. Now at 1000 feet, 800, 500. I can smell the wet grass below. At 300, I know I have no options but to land or crash onto the rocks. I suddenly see a small hill, with about a 10- 15-degree slope, plowed by a local farmer perpendicularly to the hill's slant-not recommended for landing, but is my only choice if no thermal introduces itself for a rescue. I'm still looking for a lift, sweating furiously in my cockpit. The altimeter is screaming 200 feet! I'm now committed and prepared for landing on the hill, turning sharply towards the bottom of the hill, almost touching the ground with the tip of my left wing. I level off and rotate going uphill. I did figure out that in order to land parallel to the surface, I must keep my nose very high-without an engine to help, it is a challlenging task at low speed. The glider touches down and heavily hits the plowed hill. With much relief, we stop in less than 20 feet, not without damage to the undercarriage.

I call for the retrieve.

The retrieve

I owned two gliders. The first was a DG 303 Elan, a high-performance fiber glider with a glide ratio of 40 to 1. It isa 15-meter (wingspan) beautiful sailplane that I loved flying. I later moved into an 18-meter high-performance Discus 2C T. The "T" stands for Turbo, which means a sustainer engine that saves you from landing out waiting for long retrieves. The glide ratio of the Discus exceeds 55 to 1.

In my Discus being towed at a contest in Wurtsboro, New York (N82)

All-in-all I participated in about 14 to 15 contests in several venues in the US-an experience I will never forget. I had the good fortune of meeting some of the greatest U.S. aviators, such as Neil Armstrong, Chuck Yeager, Bob Hoover, as well as George Moffat; Thomas Knauf; Karl Striedieck; Hank Nixon, and many other world-class aviators with whom I flew and raced.... and last but not least, I got to know William "Dick" Padgett (1925 - 2019). Dick was a tow pilot from as long as I remember Wurtsboro Airport (N82) to almost the last day of his life, at 93. A WWII B-17 pilot, a cigar chain-smoker who never missed an opportunity to fly, teach, or tell war stories.; how he crashed three times in enemy's territory and escaped back to his base and flew some more for his country. Although I tried endless times, he refused to give me a proper in-depth interview and tell me more about his life and experiences. A dedicated husband, father, and grandfather. May he rest in peace.

There are also races of various powered aircraft, mostly WWII warplanes; however, some races also include aircraft of Soviet-era jets and a few other qualified airplanes. The major races are performed once a year in Reno, Nevada, yet, by very experienced pilots in specialized and modified planes.

The racing planes fly between pylons posted at various distances. They fly at very low altitudes. If qualified, the emphasis is merely on speed.

Other contests focus on the maintenance and closest authenticity to the original design of a particular type. These contests are taking place in the many air shows around the USA and the world. The most popular U.S.

airshows are the EAA (Experimental Aircraft Association) Air Venture Oshkosh Air Show, attracting over 600,000 visitors to 12,000 camping sites and 10,000 visiting aircraft in a huge variety of types and makes. Other air shows are spread around the USA and other countries around the world. The following is a select venue of airshows worth attending.

Other air shows are spread around Air shows which are worth **EAA Air Venture**, Oshkosh

(KOSH),Wisconsin,the USA, with over 600,000 attendees.

Sun & Fun Air Show, Lakeland (KLAL), Florida, USA, with over 225,000 attendees.

Reno National Championship Air Races, Reno Stead (KRTS), Nevada, the USA.

The Royal International Air Tattoo boasts of being the world's largest military Air Show. RAF Fairfield, Gloucestershire, U.K.

Abbotsford Airshow, Abbotsford (CYXX), British Columbia, Canada

Wings over Camarillo Air Show, Camarillo (KCMA), California, the USA.

There are many airshows in hundreds of airports in the U.S.A. All offer a variety of Aerobatic shows, Manufacturers' showrooms exhibiting new and improved aviation products, including new and used aircraft, as well as flight schools and careers in aviation. The military finds air shows excellent venues to enlist young recruits interested in careers in aviation.

CHAPTER NINE
HE GAVE UP FIRST

Some time ago, on a beautiful spring day, I went to visit Iftach Spector at his house, and *talk shop* (his shop). "It's my inner resources that guided me through this," he said.

I found Brigadier General Spector expecting me in the backyard of his house. He was busily uprooting a dead fruit tree. He greeted me with his familiar smile and showed me to a table outside the house for the scheduled interview. As we were going there, I noticed his two-lane lap pool. He told me that, as I do, he swims laps every morning.

Spector is a triple-time Ace. An Ace, by military air jargon, is a fighter pilot credited with five confirmed air combat kills. I remember Spector as a young IAF flight instructor in the early sixties, although I never flew with him. Since then, he turned out to be one of the Air Force's legends.

I spoke to friends who knew Spector well. Most described him as a tough, demanding commander, talented in every aspect of combat flights, outspoken, intelligent, and whatnot. I think, after so many years in business, I acquired the ability to judge a person's character and qualities instantly. To me, he came through, also, as courageous, determined, and brutally honest individual. Though, I also detected traces of wit and artistic tendencies. Is that what makes a successful fighter pilot? 11 Nobody knows," he quips.

Throughout his service, Spector experienced flying on most aircraft the air force acquired. He participated in many high-profile operations, such as example, Operation Opera, the attack on the Iraqi nuclear facility, and many others. Our story, however, will revolve around one single flight in the F-4 E Phantom II.

"Fear is our body's defense mechanism against danger." He says, "Yet, I never feared during combat or during any phase of flight. Fear came to me the night before a mission or during wartime. I was especially concerned about becoming POW and about my family, my state, and my junior fighters in the squadron," Spector added.

The McDonell Douglas F-4 Phantom II, a twin-engine Fighter-Bomber, was produced between 1958 - 1980 in several variants. McDonell produced the F-4E and RF-4E in the greatest quantities of all models. In 1969 the Israel Air force (IAF) acquired about two hundred modified F-4E specimens. The IAF saw in it an answer to the intense Surface-to-

Air- Soviet-made SAM-3 Missile batteries depl.oyed by Egypt and Syria. "I found all my Phantom encounters with the enemy's MiGs quite Easy for me," claims Spector, "except for one, one-on-one combat during the Yom Kippur War.

F- 4E Phantom II	
Max Speed:	1,485 MPH (March 2.2)
Range:	1,750 Miles
Gross Weight:	55,597 lbs. (25,300 Kg)
Thrust:	2X 17,900 lbs.
Thrust to Gross Weight *Ratio*: 0.6439	
1969 Cost:	$2.4 million

I led two F-4 quartets for a bombing mission deep inside Syria. Bad luck began at the onset. When we arrived at the target, we met an atmospheric inversion of haze which completely obstructed our vision of the target. Furthermore, a bunch of MiG-21s was expecting us nearby. I realized that our mission was doomed. I ordered all participants to unload their bombs and return home to Hatzerim. By that point, we had consumed much of our fuel and all our air-to-ground payload."

The US Navy needed a plane that was capable of intercepting Soviet intruders at high altitudes. The Pentagon then ordered the F-4 Phantom for the Navy, which to this day still holds impressive records. Among those records climbing to the high-altitude record of 98,600 ft utilizing a climb rate of more than 41,000 ft/min. Since the Pentagon believed that cannons in fighters were a "thing of another era," its engineers denied it a cannon. Yet, made it rely on four AIM-7E and four AIM 9B, Air-to-Air missiles for air interception-as a "modern concept for air superiority." When complaints from McDonell's customers were piling up, the manufacturer added the 20mm, M61Al Vulcan Gatling cannon to aid in air-to-air combats when needed.

"The MiGs we saw above our target in Syria decided to attack us on our way home. As I instructed, we tried to avoid them the best we could. Regardless, on a quick head count, we discovered that we are missing Dubbie Joffe, one of our team members. I was furious! Not only that our mission had failed, but we also lost a pilot and a good plane."

"As our Phantoms were quite light at that phase, I figured that our ratios must have also improved against the MiG-21, but the MiG had its own advantages; we were not driving a quick and agile Mirage and, with limited fuel in our tanks. In any event, this was no excuse whatsoever to break the iron-clad rule 'not to engage in any side adventure,' no less in air combat on the wayhome. A rule which I instilled ferociously in my squadron."

"I noticed a single MiG-21 making attack maneuvers against our straight-lined-up convoy."

"At that moment, I broke all the rules! The day's accumulated frustration and especially what I believed was a useless loss of a mate, my anger, took hold of me. The Mirage-jockey attributes captured my judgment, 'childish as it was.' I turned my Phantom's nose towards the MiG and began one-on-one engagement maneuvers."

"Personally, I am not an aggressive individual. I avoid confrontations, and as a child and a young adult, I was never hurt or got hurt by anyone. In the air, I had other challenges to confront."

"The other Phantoms were on their way home. Erel,. my Weapon and Systems Officer (WSO), and I remained deep in Syria with limited remaining fuel against that single MiG. And so, the combat began. I quickly realized that this was not going to be easy. The Syrian pilot is the best opponent I ever faced, and in fact, he was as skilled as I was-this will be a battle for life or death, I concluded."

With his extra energy, he turned around and closed on us from a back. I then lifted my nose to about twenty degrees and performed a modified slow Aileron Roll, attempting to 'let him pass' and take his position on his six. This surprised him, but being an excellent pilot, as he was, he pulled and reduced his own speed. I was quite amazed at his quick response. He was flying right next to us at a dead slow speed. At this point, both our noses pointed up, probablyat their critical AOAs and at their imminent-stall speeds.

We were on the eastern slope of a tall mountain, only a few feet from the ground. Erel drew my attention to the hole our engines dug in the ground with the fire coming out of their exhausts. My plane was shaking violently, attempting to unsuccessfully hold the low altitude that we were at. I am sweating nervously, and lots of butterflies are roaming my belly. Erel senses my emotional state and, in an almost whispering voice, attempts to calm me down, calling me to relax; 'relax, Iftach, relax.'

"We are in a vertical rolling Scissors." 'Scissors' is a maneuver that aims at slowing the aircraft down to maintain its position behind the opponent. Technically, it is done by flying a slow barrel roll around the opponent's flight path. "I know that whoever tries to get out of this maneuver is going to enter the opponent's cannon or missile zones or simply spin to the ground." All the warning lights are red, and the plane is screaming 'stall' and 'terrain' warnings while shaking like a leaf. The fuel gauges are scary to look at, realizing their implications. I wish I could shut one engine off and save some of that precious liquid. All the while, both the MiG and us slowly slide back toward the ground. The radio, too, is busy calling frantically, God knows whom or what. 'Relax, Iftach, relax/ chants Erel from the back.

By now, I am tensed and drained from the energy spent. My suit is soaking wet with sweat, and the rubber, hydraulic oil, and the entire cockpit scent play havoc on my stomach." We are in a tough situation, to say the least. Both us and the MiG are at a minimum speed and on the verge of crashing on our tail at the bottom of that hill. I am flying the plane with the tip of my fingers, as delicately as I can-the wrong move will kill us. I am totally focused on my Phantom's abilities to help me stay in a good defensive position. My fuel gauges look awful.

Suddenly, a miracle, "our opponent pilot lost his cool posture that he had held all this while. His MiG had moved ahead of us vertically, then flipped towards us, almost crashing on top of us. Then, we observed the pilot ejects and falls to the ground, his spinning plane following and crashing on top of him. Not a pleasant observation!"

I breathe freely and turn slowly away from the Syrian mountain, west, towards home. I did not talk, there was nothing to be said, and none of us wished to interrupt the unwinding of our tensions. I shut off one engine and cruised toward the awesome sight of the sinking sun.

Tomorrow, I will have to explain my rowdy behavior to my other pilots at the squadron.

Looking closely at both the F-4 Phantom II and the MiG-2l's capabilities, I find them to be awfully close and typical to interceptors of that era. Although the Phantom was much heavier and much more cumbersome compared to the MiG (or the Mirage), it had enormous power plants, which helped it compensate. It kept the Thrust-to-Empty-Weight ratio much more favorable with its powerful engines. All other attributes were almost identical, but the MiG had a few advantages for air combat. Yet, I have no doubt in my mind that the difference lies in those riding them. The skills and the ability to control your temper in tough situations are paramount. This, I believe, is what won Spector the day.

Those traits are true in every type of flying, especially in emergencies. Keep flying, and stay cool. I would be a miss if I ended this chapter without paying tribute to two people that I hold dear. My friend Pini Nachmani, a Phantom Weapon Systems Officer (WSO) who served 5 years in a Syrian prison after ejecting into enemy territory, and Shmuel

Hetz, another brilliant phantom pilot whose plane was shot down by an Egyptian missile. As my flight instructor, Hetz taught me how to fly.

"If we win here, we will win everywhere. The world is a fine place and worth fighting for...."

Ernest Hemingway (For Whom the Bell Tolls)

CHAPTER TEN
IN THE FOOTSTEPS OF
HARRY, THE CUTTER

My fascination with the Mustang began at fourteen, a few decades ago. I was in an air force-sponsored youth club back when the P-51's aura still filled the air. We constructed models of gliders and other aircraft. Of all models, my favorite was the Mustang. Its popularity among us was ahead of other WWII legends such as the British Spitfire or Republic's P-47 ... and not without reason; its superior performance made it the best fighter of its era. I must have built two or three Mustang balsa models, painstakingly crafted. Some years after, they were stiII hanging out in my room at my parent's house. The Mustang's design (concept to prototype completed in a mere 120 days) was unquestionably captivating. I loved it and was intimately familiar with every curve and angle,every detail, and all specs and data available in those days forth is intriguing aircraft... long before I was even near one. Initially, the Mustang, then designated NA-73, was developed by North American Aviation for the British Purchasing Commission, which also gave it its famous Mustang designation. There were over 15,000 Mustangs manufactured by North American Aviation between 1940 and 1945, and, at peak, a rate of over

800 planes per month was built, most of them awaiting newly trained pilots. In later years, I had the opportunity to closely examine a couple of remnants of the Israel Air Force's (IAF) famous P-51 Squadron Scorpion at an Air Force base, but a live introduction to this legendary plane remained a dream.

IAF Mustang P-51D

Major Harry Karsenstein was an Australian World War II fighter pilot who, in 1948, during Israel's war of independence, volunteered to join and fly for the fledgling IAF. Karsenstein (later changed to Barak) carried on serving in the IAF and was my first-solo examiner and a frequent instructor in IAF flight school. I remember him to be a tall, handsome individual, wearing a typical RAF (Royal Air Force) mustache on his always-tanned face. He was a reserved, no-nonsense pilot and a decidedly demanding flight instructor. Most of the time, during dual flights, he would sit in the back quietly or sporadically mutter something unintelligible. When he spoke, it was with a heavy foreign accent, which for us was, at times, quite difficult to comprehend. Worse still were his pronunciations of names. By the time I had the privilege of knowing him, he was already an IAF legend.

As one of the stories goes, at the onset of the 1956 Suez Affair, Karsenstein's P-51 reserve-pilot squadron, Scorpion, was assigned the mission of destroying the enemy's communication lines along the Suez Canal and the Sinai desert before pursuing air and ground attacks were launched. Flying in pairs, the improvised technique was to drag a boom, tied by a 200-yard cable to the Mustang's tail, across telephone wires, thus tearing them apart. Scorpion's mission was critical to the campaign's success. Leaving communication lines open would rob the ground forces of the element of surprise, which could have been disastrous in terms of human lives and equipment loss. In late October, departing at dawn, Karsenstein and his wingman sped at deck altitude across the sleepy desert towards the Canal. Arriving before the guards were even awakened, they worked the wires until Karsenstein's boom snapped loose. Frustrated and anxious to complete his mission successfully, he roared down toward the wires and cut every last one of them with his Mustang's huge and powerful propeller and wings! The mission was an enormous success, and from that day on, Harry Karsenstein was dubbed *Harry the Cutter*.

My numerous attempts to get him to speak about the many fables attributed to his days at Scorpion Squadron were only met with more impatient mutterings. Major Karsenstein was responsible, though, for the nickname that stuck with me for years. One day, at a field we used for training, a Piper Cub piloted by 'Simmle,' a buddy of mine crashed nose-down on the runway. Returning to the field from a training solo flight and already on a short final, I was signaled to abort the landing. Yet, like any other eighteen-year-old, I continued my descent until just over the heads of crews and spectators, leaving the site in a *roaring buzz*. When I eventually landed and was back on the line, Karsenstein, sitting in a field service truck, popped up his head and yelled out, "Eddie, you are grounded," without further explanation. The guys on the ramp rolled on the floor laughing hysterically, and from that day, I was known to all as "Eddie."

For me, the Mustang and Karsenstein were bundled in one mysterious package. My curiosity into Karsenstein's past at Scorpion Squadron had to be satisfied by others, and a glimpse into the rest of the package was yet to come.

A month ago, I had a conversation with an aviation friend in New Mexico. The conversation turned to the Mustang, and I asked him if he knew of any operation where I could fly one. He immediately directed me to Lee Lauderback at Stallion 51 of Kissimmee, Florida. I was quite excited at the prospect of finally fulfilling an old dream and suggested to my wife we drive to our Florida house and stop on the way in Kissimmee. She agreed, and I called Lee to make the arrangements.

Lee runs Stallion 51 Corporation and its flight operation, and his twin brothers, Richard and Peter, operate the restoration and maintenance program they offer to their customers... They own Crazy Horse, a North American TF-51 Mustang. They also restore and manage several other warplanes for a variety of avid collectors, as well as participate in air shows and train U.S. Air Force pilots to fly the TF-51. For the First Flight Centennial they trained for a fly-by formation flight of Crazy Horse alongside U.S. Air Force F-15, F-16, and A-10 jet fighters.

As planned, we arrived in Kissimmee at noon and were greeted by Sharon, who proudly showed us around. I had never seen such an immaculate facility and equipment: the aircraft at the hangar, four P-51D Mustangs, two TF-51 Mustangs, and a Spitfire looked just like toy models in a store's window. All are painted in authentic squadron colors and markings and kept spotless. There was not a drop of oil or a speck of dust on the hangar's polished floor. The picture-perfect scene could have only been replicated in a museum. After the quick tour, I was led to a conference room where Lee was awaiting me.

Lee began flying gliders at fourteen and, over the years, accumulated a couple of thousand hours flying and instructing gliders. In the eighties, he got involved with Mustangs and, ever since, accumulated over five thousand hours in them, flying, instructing, and certifying Mustang pilots. Lee does things well; one can tell. And there is no question that he loves what he does. Crazy Horse is the TF-51 Mustang he uses to train pilots and the one I'm going to fly. It is a single-seat P-51D fighter, modified to a two-seater, dual control fighter-trainer.

After an investigation into my flying experience, Lee begins his preflight briefing for the TF-51 - her performance, flying characteristics, instruments, and emergency procedures. "Apparently," Lee remarks,

"North American Aviation never produced a two-seater model, and the lack of such a trainer resulted in more pilot loss during training than in actual combat." Its powerful 1650 HP Rolls Royce Merlin 68 engine provides the plane with exceptional performance, from vertical climb to a maximum speed of 437 MPH at 25,000 ft, and an amazing 7.3 knots climb rate to nearly 42,000 ft of service ceiling. Its payload, as flown in WWII, exceeded 4,500 lbs. (empty weight 7,635 lbs.) to a combat range of some 2,000 SM, with drop tanks. "During the war, she was flown at her maximum weight of 12,100/lbs. But today, we'll be flying her at approximately 8,200 lbs." says Lee.

This kind of performance is quite remarkable, even by today's standards. Combine this huge power plant with the ingenious aerodynamics and structural design of the aircraft, and you get outstanding maneuverability, evidenced by the extraordinary number of kills and ground support missions it performed during its service.

" ...You'll be flyingthe plane, and I'll talk you into each procedure. We'll begin with taxiing and takeoff. We'll do some basic stuff, such as steep turns and slow flight, a few stalls, and then more complex maneuvers and aerobatics, concluding with an overhead break and a full stop landing," Lee explains. "We'll have about 0.70 hours to do it."

The weather appears to be ideal for this kind of flight. Ground temperature is unusually cool at 55° F, blue sky as far as the eye can see; a light northwesterly wind with very stable air aloft, and visibility of at least 60 miles in all directions.

We walk toward Crazy Horse, who is waiting for us in full colors and all her glory. My heart is pounding hard, and all my senses are on full alert with expectation. I can only compare the experience to a reunion with your high school sweetheart or with a once best friend - only *she* hasn't changed. We stop next to her, and I feast my eyes on all those parts I'm so familiar with. Nothing is different. She's an exact *replica of all my Mustang models* ... as beautiful as I remembered her to be. I think Lee senses the dramatic event and lets me seize the moment without interruption.

We climb into the cockpit, and Lee begins to show me around. The back seat is a duplicate of the front except for some controls (including the gear lever, fuel selection, radio dials, and navigation systems essential for solo flights). There are three video cameras: one located on the horizontal stabilizer's leading edge, another on top of the vertical stabilizer, and a third in the cockpit, facing the pilot in the back seat. The instructor controls each camera to correspond with the appropriate maneuver the aircraft flies. At the debriefing, the tape is viewed, and the flight gets analyzed. I get into the backseat, and Lee helps me reach the straps and hands me a helmet and earplugs. I connect the intercom and make myself comfortable. There is one thing absent, though-the smell of hydraulic fluid or of sun-scorched rubber, typically present in military piston-fighters. The instruments are modern, up-to-date, and easily within reach, except for the flaps' handle, which is impossibly located at the far back end to your left. The cockpit is immaculately maintained and all in tip-top condition. Lee straps in and goes over the checklist as fast as he can move his lips. C L E A R, the engine coughs, ejects a heap of smoke and starts humming in rhythm, bringing the entire frame into life in perfect harmony. So well-adjusted is it that the instrument panel doesn't vibrate or shake a bit during all the locomotion. We check ATIS. I note the information and adjust the altimeter to the pressure altitude.

"Let's taxi to runway 33 and stop *before takeoff* check. You have the aircraft." Taxiing is a bit tricky in a tail dragger and especially from the back seat of a long-nosed aircraft like the Mustang.

All the whille, you keep the stick in a forward position to relieve weight from the tail wheel. Still, I manage, and we get to runway 33 and stop for the takeoff check. I rev the engine to 2300 RPM, check magnetos, manifold pressure, engine oil, and hydraulic pressure, and we're ready to go!

Kissimmee tower, Mustang 0 1, ready for takeoff," calls Lee.

"Mustang Zero-One clear to go," prompts the tower in a crispy matter-of-fact tone .... Mustang sounds so unbelievable! We line up on the runway, increase power to 30 inches of manifold pressure, and release the brakes. At 50 knots, we bring up the tail and increase power to 55 inches.

Vertical climb as viewed from the cockpit

She rushes along and, at 100 knots, takes off with little effort.

We level off at 7,000 over a training area some thirty miles south of the airport. I first try some steep turns, then slow flight. I realize how stable and controllable the Mustang is. You hardly need any rudder in the turns, and the airplane reacts promptly and smoothly to the control movements at 300 knots. I then reduce the speed to nearly 80 knots for slow flight, bring the nose up further, and at some 72 knots, she stalls and drops a left-wing. I recover, and Lee explains that the Mustang would drop a corresponding wing with the smallest deflection of the rudder. The next stall was straightforward.

I find *Wing* Over maneuver more difficult than it appears to observers. You find a reference on the ground, lower the nose a bit, and then raise the pitch altitude toward the horizon. As it approaches the horizon, you begin to add a bank to the left (or right), and by the time you have turned a 90° heading change, you bleed much of your speed in a 90° bank. At this point, you apply the top stick in a coordinated turn and go down, repeating the maneuver over. Again, perfectly performed.

Aileron and barrel rolls were a breeze for the Mustang, though, naturally, not as swift as a much faster jet. "Try her in a loop," suggests Lee. "Enter at 260 knots and pull steady about 3 Gs." I bring the nose down a few degrees, and she quickly gets to the desired speed. I pull 3-4 Gs and look straightforward. Although a 3-G pull isn't much stress, if you were ever engaged in aggressive aerobatics, you'd instinctively tense your stomach and other voluntary muscles upon application of any positive G to reduce blood drainage from your head. First comes the sky, beginning with the light blue of the horizon into the deeper blue as the aircraft is in its vertical position, then the earth colors move above, and the light-blue horizon is up-front, as we are inverted .. I reduce the pressure on the stick, reaching almost zero Gs at the top, and experience the familiar drop-into-the-seatbelt effect. I smile to myself and let the aircraft dive the blue above with the beautiful colors of Florida below, increasing the pull and leveling at the horizon. I always feel great after recovery from a medium to high G application. With the rush of oxygen back to the brain, there is a high that gets you somewhat euphoric. This time is no different. But then, I awake to the still more ecstatic reality that, this time, I'm in no less than a P-51 Mustang.

Over the years, I have flown several militaries and general aviation aircraft, modern and old, including my own high-performance gliders and airplanes. I have done this maneuver in jets, gliders, as well as other modern aircraft. The ageless Mustang did it as smoothly and elegantly as any one of them!

"Well, what'd you think of the Mustang so far?" Lee throws in to the intercom.

"She's amazing," I say and add nothing more.

"Are you OK?" Lee checks on me.

'I'm fine," I reply, thinking, *what does he think I'm made of?... I'll get sick when I'm good and ready.*

"Well then,"he says, "how about a Cuban Eight?"

"Sure," I reply.

"Keep the RPM and Manifold pressure where it is and stay at your 260 knots for the entry."

"Yep," I acknowledge and stop for a second to look around and scan the instruments.

I have no idea where Karsenstein is today, but now, some forty-odd years later, inside a Mustang and in the air, I am beginning to see, feel, and live some of the passionate moments that he and the Mustang must have shared.

Again, I add backpressure to 3 Gs toward the *rainbow of blues* and slow at the *drop-into-the-harness* position, inverted in the middle of the sky.

A left aileron and a tiny opposite rudder to half a turn recover the aircraft to normal attitude. I apply forward pressure to gain back entry speed and pull back hard to the top. *Drop-into-the-seatbelts.* Half a turn and I'm rapidly back to the mosaic of the earth at leveled and normal flying attitude.

Years ago, I was told that because of its huge V-12 engine, the torque effect in the Mustang is quite vicious, and you need to constantly counter it with a right rudder to keep it stable. I must admit that except for takeoff and some tiny, odd corrections at flight, the *ball* is almost always centered, and deviation is hardly felt. So far, she is a remarkably stable, easily trimmed, friendly, and easy-flying machine.

Time's up, and we start toward the airport. Lee requests permission for an overhead break at 500 ft, "The lowest they will permit," he explains, as I'm thinking, *A bit of a difference from my 50-foot overhead break years ago.* We go back to a thousand over the runway.

I pull hard with a sharp left turn downwind of the active runway. At 240 knots, we bring the flaps to 20°, reduce speed to 150, drop the gear and flaps to 30°, and turn base, dropping the flaps further to 40° and turning final. Drop flaps to full, and I keep 110 through the threshold, reducing further to 100 knots and flare... touch down... oops, balloon slightly, then rest her steady on the runway and taxi to the hangar.

Whew ... what a stormy experience.

Landing back on runway 33, I get out of the cockpit when I spot my wife taking pictures. She later noted the big grin on my face.

Tomorrow I'll go back to my glider. To ride the winds... chase buzzards and hawks, rejoin the dazzling dance with nature, in complete serenity and satisfaction of yet another dream, fulfilled...

This article was first published in the EAA Warbird Magazine.

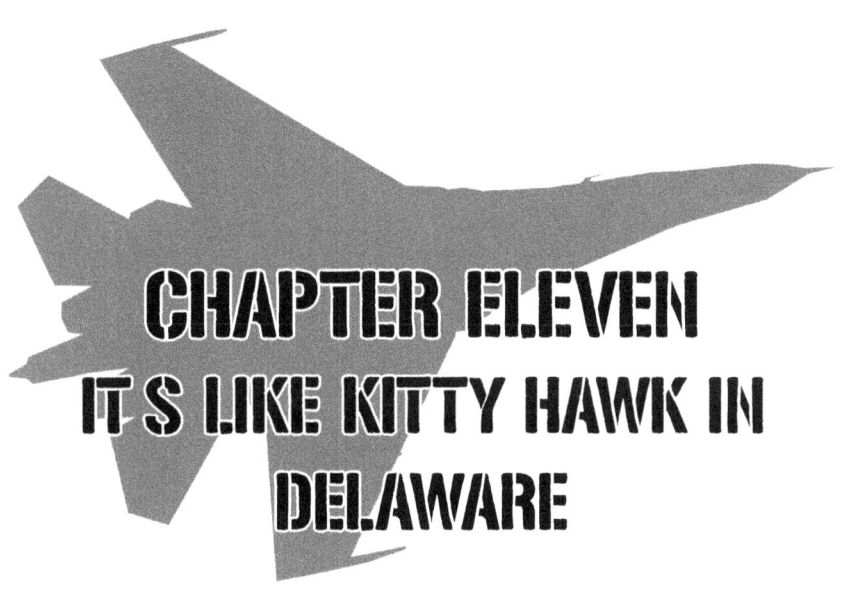

CHAPTER ELEVEN
IT'S LIKE KITTY HAWK IN
DELAWARE

*T*he two jets stood in formation at the edge of the runway, engines blasting
and raring to go. "Formation Black and Red taking off runway 01...."

"Good flying, Black and Red." The two charged forward simultaneously
and, with a thundering roar, rushed to consume the shortest possible distance
on the runway. By the time Red reached its rotation speed, Black was already
passing through a thousand feet of altitude.

Joe Gano had invited me to come down and test-fly his Viper version of
the L-29 Delfin. "The Viper L-29," he says, "it's like no other L-29, L-39,
or any other jet trainer in its class." *Big statement*, I thought, and replied,
"I'm no test pilot, Joe, but just for the fun of it, I'd love to participate."

L-29 Viper over Wilmington

In the mid-1960s, the Czech Aero L-29 Delfin won several design competitions initiated by the Soviet Union for its members. It was found to be an excellent basic trainer: easy to operate and simple to fly. It had docile handling characteristics, could be operated from grass, sand, or waterlogged strips, and was equipped with provisions to carry light armament. For all these reasons and its reliability (the lack of which could get you sent to Siberia), the Soviets found it ideal for their training programs. They ordered the L-29 in massive numbers. Its original prototype was powered by the British Bristol Siddelley Viper turbojet, but as Rolls Royce refused to supply the engine to the Soviets, all 3,600 L-29 copies produced by 1974 were equipped, with some modifications, with the Motorlet M 701c 500 powerplant, rated at 1,962 lbs. of thrust.

The Viper L-29 is an entirely different animal. It's the brainchild of Dave Cannavo, a man who literarily spent all his 50 years around airplanes, becoming a brilliant engineer and superior test pilot.

It all began at home. His dad had owned and operated an FBO and charter operation at New Castle County Airport. "The place was nothing like this," Dave confided, "but it hummed with airplanes. I was around them as far back as I can remember. At one time, we owned as many as seventeen aircraft, and I was tinkering with aircraft parts from an early age. By the time I was thirteen, I was overhauling Pratt & Whitney engines on Beech 18s, and as soon as I got old enough, I got my rating. My dad never forced me to do any of this," he continues, "I just loved doing it."

And love it. He did. At the age of nineteen, Dave "had the urge"to build an exact replica of the Ryan NYP Spirit of St. Louis. In his research, he found Ed Morrow, an eighty-year-old retired sheet metal specialist who had worked on the original plane. "They never made a set of blueprints for that aircraft." Dave explains, shaking his head. It was only a few months after that historic flight that Morrow put together a set of plans to match a pile of scrap paper with sketches drawn by Donald Hall, Lindbergs engineer, as they built the plane to Lindberg's specifications. "So, I bought a set of his plans."

But those blueprints were only half the solution. They were not very accurate, and parts wouldn't fit. "I contacted the Smithsonian and asked to examine the Spirit of St. Louis up close, "says Dave. "They agreed, and I made two trips, very early, before visiting hours began, and took Cannavo's 1978 replica of Spirit of St. Luis hundreds of pictures of every part of the aircraft. I ended up working a great deal with those pictures."

After three years on the project, working nights and weekends, an exact replica of the Spirit of St. Louis was born, except for the engine, which Dave decided to replace with a more reliable 225 HP Lycoming R-680. On Thanksgiving Day of 1978, Dave and a couple of friends brought the plane to Philadelphia International ("They practically closed the airport for us"), and when they taxi-tested the aircraft, "the plane just took off." Dave flew it for ten minutes to the fanfare of reporters and enthusiasts, then brought it back home to New Castle County Airport. He logged additional 250 hours before he abandoned a plan to cross the Atlantic "only for the lack of time." In 1995, N- X- 211 was sold to Kermit Weeks of the Fantasy of Flight Museum in Polk City, Florida, where, to this day, it is displayed and occasionally flown.

Sometime last fall, I visited Dave at his home.

Cruising up a winding driveway on his 280-acre property, I reached the top, and without much warning, there emerged an aviator's wonderland -- a 3700 ft grass landing strip, surrounded by aircraft of every kind, some assembled and ready to fly, some in parts, and some huge crates just arrived for a new assembly.

Dave and an unassembled L-39

There were a couple of SU-25, an L-39 or two, a colorful Yak-18T, two Antonov AN-2s, two or three L-295, a MiG-21, a Beech 18, a Cessna 172, MiG-23, some 12 Canadian F-5, and whatnot. Next to a beautiful house atop the hill stood a hangar two stories high, crammed with a variety of aircraft in various stages of modification and assembly. "We shipped over three dozen L-39s and scores of L-29s from this place before we got into the supersonic fighters and the L-29 Viper project," Dave told me. It all began when visiting the Air & Space Museum at Kbely in the Czech Republic, when Colonel Remek, the museum director, blurted, "I'd swap an L-29 and and a MiG-21, for a DC-3..."

Dave's backyard

"It's a deal," said Dave without a moment's hesitation. "Only later did I begin to realize the extent of the preparations needed to fly a 180-mph aircraft with limited internal fuel, inadequate navigation systems, and a crew that never flew a DC-3, across the Atlantic and all the way to Prague?" But he did it. He found a DC-3 operating as an air cargo somewhere in the Midwest, devised a six-tank, 1200-gallon auxiliary fuel supply, placing them three at the aft and three at the front of the CG, got himself type-rated, and off he went on a 24-hour flight to consummate the deal. "The Czechs couldn't believe their eyes when we landed there," said Dave. "We made this very deal six different times before," they said, and no one could come close to delivering. I stayed several more days to watch them disassemble my airplanes and to study the MiG's systems." This delivery of the L-29 and MiG-21 to the U.S. was followed by many other Soviet- (and Russian) era jet fighters -- including the only U.S. registered, certified, and flying MiG-23 Flogger and a soon-to-be-certified Sukhoi SU-25 Frogfoot. Realizing that the stock L-29 Delfin was designed for and could house the Viper engine, which would vastly improve the stock L-29 performance, Dave decided to start the L-29 Viper project.

What he created is an L-29 with 3340 lbs. of thrust and a thrust/weight ratio of 0.47. More than 23% better than that of the L-39 Albatross, better than the Alpha Jet, or even the A- 10 Thunderbolt, and almost twice that of the L-29 Delfin.

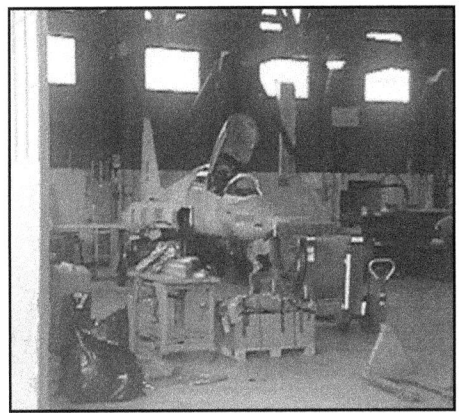 

Restoring Canadian F-5   Dave, I, and the Viper

Maximum speed increased from 350 (235 cruising) to 435 knots (300 NM cruising), ranging from 300 to 420 miles at 18,000 ft, and sustaining g, at 10,000 ft, from 2.3 to 5.5. Dave put it to me this way: "If you get two equally good pilots flying the two airplanes [the L-29 Viper and L-39 Albatros], the Viper will go out vertical the 39 right up to 40,000 ft. He will also outturn the L-39, so there will be no place for it to hide in the aircombat envelope. Should the L-39 start air combat while sitting on the Viper's tail, the Viper will outmaneuver it every time with a simple loop, split-s, or a break." His statements intrigued me, and I decided to put them to the test in my forthcoming test flight, pushing the challenge a little further; I would invite my friend Giera Epstein to help settle the wager. Brigadier General Epstein, a retired fighter pilot and squadron commander in the Israeli Air Force, with seventeen jet kills (mostly of MiG-21s), is the world's uncontested Ace of all Aces. Epstein logged over 25,000 flight hours, 5,000 flying military aircraft,. including the Mirage IIIC, IAI Daggers, IAI Kfirs, F-4 Phantoms, and F-16 Falcons (with over 500 combat missions), and some 20,000 hours in commercial aircraft from Boeing 707 to the 777. I figured we'd put Epstein in the stock L-29

Delfin with Tom Riley (a high-hours L-29 flyer) as his safety pilot and Joe Gano, the college tuition banker, with myself the Private Equity banker in the L-29 Viper. If the bankers outperform the Pro flyers, the Viper would be, without a doubt, crowned the superior aircraft.

The Author (right), Epstein, and his ride

It is a beautiful early-October day in Wilmington. Temperatures are in the mid-seventies, scattered clouds at 7,000 ft, and the wind are blowing from the northwest at 5 to 8 knots. Everyone's gathered at the airport for the occasion. My wife and I arrived the night before with Giora Epstein and his wife, Sarah. Joe Gano, Dave Cannavo, Tom Riley, the ground crew, and a couple of close friends met us there. The air was charged with anticipation, and the mix of all-aviator participants and spectators made for great chemistry. To warm up and begin to feel out each of the aircraft, I'm to take a flight with Dave in the stock L-29, and then both crews will man their planes and proceed to positions on the runway. We are to takeoff in formation, each at our best rate of climb, and meet by the water tower, 10 miles northeast of the airport at 5,000 ft. Above the assigned waypoint, we are to regroup, gather speed, and climb vertically to zero-indicated airspeed, then finally level off and accelerate to maximum speed.

The pre-flight with Dave was a lot of fun. I flew the L-39 a couple of years ago and loved it, but I'd never flown the L-29. I found the L-29 extremely simple to operate and very easy to fly. It is docile, smooth, and quick to react, with very similar characteristics, although less zest, than the L-39. After a series of maneuvers and some play, we continued 30 miles southwest of the airport and buzzed Dave's house at 30ft AGL and 250 knots to "wake the kids up." Though I flew the aircraft most of the time, Dave's 11,000 hours and lifetime experience gave the flight in this jet warbird a whole new dimension. Meanwhile, back at the ranch, Black

Viper readied for the formation flight. Red was refueled as soon as we landed, and the wives were giggling and taking pictures.

It's that time! We slip into the cockpits, plug our headsets in and prepare for the ride-*no G- suits, helmets, or oxygen masks for these cowboys!* We start the engines, communicate with the tower, and taxi to our positions on the runway. Joe and I are in the lead, and Red is positioned some twenty-five yards behind on the other side of the runway. We signal Red to rev up and push the throttle to the metal. Engine at 100%, hand squeezed on the brake handle. A quick glance at the gauges, engine temperature, and pressures. Like a pit bull on a leash, the Viper vibrates and shakes, yearning to charge forward. I glance at Red. A stream of hot fumes is expelled from its engine in a trail of vapor and haze. Giora and Tom look preoccupied, surveying their own panel. We radio the tower, get their blessings, and then signal Red our OK for takeoff. We release the brakes, and the Viper charges forward at accelerating speed. The dividing marks on the runway below rush exceedingly faster and grow smaller as the Viper leaps to the sky at one-third of the runway. Within seconds, we cross one thousand feet of altitude. "I lost them!" I tell Joe. "They are still on the runway," he replies, not without amusement.

In fact, Red just left the ground, using two-thirds of the runway.

Dave's allegations start to sink in ... *It's amazing how different the Viper is,* I'm thinking, as we circle around our next rendezvous, waiting for Red to make it up here.

"Black Viper at 425 knots."

"Red 29 at 300, going home."

"Red, seventy-four-foxtrot, Black, alpha-delta at your 3 o'clock circling counterclockwise over the target at 5000," calls Joe'

Have you in sight, black alpha-delta."

"We'll be heading 180. Join us and lead, accelerating to 250 at exactly 5,000. On my signal, climb vertically through a hole in the clouds." "Roger, Black Viper, will do." I see Red in the corner of my left eye as they inch into the lead. "Please call your altitude when you break the dimb," I remind them. "Roger, Black, will do," Red repeats. "Here's a hole, just ahead, get ready, and... pull!" Here we go! We pull about 4 g to vertical attitude, straight into the deep blue of the sky. From my peripheral vision, I note the land beneath us receding in a hurry, and clouds are passing by at an even greater rate. For a moment Red is about 50 yards to our left and slightly ahead until we begin to swallow altitude, pass them, and lose sight. "Red breaking at 7500 feet, zero indicated airspeed," we hear the announcement on the frequency. *Wow, I think we are at 9,450, some 2,000 feet ahead of Red, with 170 KIAS still left. The bankers are winning, big time!* Now at 12,000, we radio, "We'll meet you at 10,000." A sharp break and a roll to the left, and speed brakes slightly open, bring the Viper next to Red and in the lead. "Go to the max and return home. We will announce maximum speed." "Roger, we're opening now." Once again, we push the throttle to the max, and within seconds, we reach 400 knots.

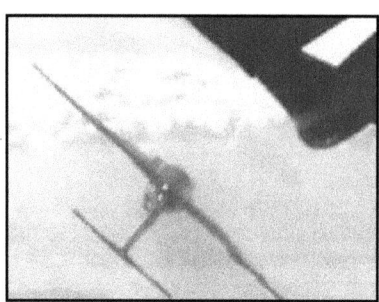

I glance at the fuel gauge. We still have 100 gallons or so. We make a steep 360° turn at 250 knots and easily sustain 5 G throughout the turn without losing speed or altitude.

"Should the L-39 start an air combat while sitting on the Viper's tail, the Viper will outmaneuver it every time with a simple loop, split-s, or a break."

I have no illusions that my skills or Joe's, either individually or combined, equal anything close to Epstein's flying skills; therefore, besides being easy and fun to fly, the Viper has superior attributes in every respect. Hurray to Dave.

7.5 G on the meter

We land, and as soon as we're parked, I jump out, shake Dave's hand, and congratulate him on a great engineering product. The wives are still giggling and taking pictures.

A few years later, I found out, to my dismay, that Dave passed away at age 63. The aviation world lost another genius.

CHAPTER TWELVE
MIG-21: BEYOND THE MYTH
AND THE LEGENDS

Accounts from the Ace of Aces

Performance means initiative-the most valuable moral and practical asset in any form of war.

Major Sholto Douglas, Royal Air Force

J oe called Thursday afternoon and announced that Sunday's flight was a go. "The aircraft is ready, and the forecast for Sunday looks quite good. Pre-flight briefing at 09:00 hours," he said. I couldn't believe I was about to fly the most formidable jet fighter the Western World had to confront on so many grounds and for so many years.

Retired Captain Joe Gano, a successful businessman and former USAF F-102 fighter pilot of the sixties, called my office one morning and, in a matter-of-fact tone, said, "How would you like to ride a MiG twenty-one?"

When I finished gathering myself off the floor, I replied calmly, "Sure, let me think about it for a day or two...." We continued to chat for an hour or so, exchanging airplane stories, and before I hung up, I said, heart still trembling, "Yeah, I think I would like to make a couple of flights on the 21, especially if I can get some input from aces who flew against it in actual combat. It would make a good story," figuring I can secure this self-imposed condition quite easily. Little did I know I would manage to enlist the world's *Ace of all Aces* for the mission. We made a deal. I hung up and jumped in the air, real high.

Although he did not participate in actual combat, young Captain Gano accumulated over 1,250 hours, largely in simulated intercepts opposite F-4 Phantoms, F-104 Starfighters, F-86 Sabres, British Lightnings, F-102s, and other fighters of that time. Much of it "informally:" After a Twenty-five-year hiatus, Joe decided to dabble back into some serious flying. And he went for it, all out. With the help of his buddy Dave Cannavo, an engineer, and a brilliant mechanic, he purchased and restored a little squadron of his own. The fleet, dubbed Warbirds of Delaware, includes three MiG-21s, two MiG-23, and a variety of other specimens from the Soviet era.

Wilmington Airport is about two hours away from my home, and I showed up at Aero Taxi Enterprises' terminal, the home of Warbirds of Delaware, at 09:00 hours as instructed. Joe and the rest of the crew were already waiting there. "We are going to fly 0165, the UM, two-sitter MiG- 21," Joe informed me. "It's parked outside. Go take a look.,.,

The delta-winged Mikoyan-Gurevich MiG-21UM model is the fighter trainer equivalent of the MiG-21MF, designated Fishbed-J by NATO. Both were manufactured in the Czech Republic by order of the Soviet Air Force. The 21MF has 14,550 pounds of thrust and a weight of 16,610 lbs.

(0.875 T /W ratios), including internal fuel. It is twice supersonic with a maximum speed of 1,353 mph and wing loading of some 87.5 lbs./SF. Its service ceiling is an impressive 58,000 ft, with an amazing climb rate of 36,900 ft/min in combat gear; it is armed with one twin-barrel 23mm cannon and two Atoll AA-2 air-to-air missiles. It may appear crude, but it's a tough aircraft, designed to operate from rough fields and unfinished strips almost anywhere. The composition of its hardened exterior was, for years, an unsolved mystery in the West. Although it lacks the finesse of an American or French fighter, it certainly looks very intimidating.

"Let's make this flight an introduction," I suggest. "I'd like to feel the aircraft out and see where I can find some discernable weaknesses in performance." I'll present the findings to our Aces and compare results with their actual performance in combat."

"That's great," said Joe, "we can then fly again and see how it plays out." Joe briefs me on the characteristics of the 21. We discuss ejection procedures, performance, and Joe's own experience flying the aircraft. I sense that Joe is apprehensive about ejecting, if it should ever come to that, and would rather try to force-land the aircraft. Seeing that so many pilots bailed out of the MiG 21 successfully, I do not agree. Before we leave for the plane, he lends me a life vest and his USAF service-day hellmet for the flight. It is a nice day--great visibility, very stable cool air with hardly any wind-a perfect day for our flight. We are to fly VFR, and our ceiling will be restricted to the Class A, 18,000 ft floor. I climb into the cockpit and have just minutes to study its interior before Joe is set to start the engine. Most of the instruments are westernized, but some are still the former Soviet design. I buckle up and lock the seatbelts and parachute. I connect the oxygen hose and plug in the communication cord. We do not wear G-suits. In an emergency, the ejection of both seats gets activated by either one of the pilots.

I mentally position the ejection handles and check the oxygen flow and the intercom. I then set the altimeter to the field elevation and the directional indicator to the magnetic compass. Visibility from the back seat is quite restricted, and I'm hoping that, from the front seat, Joe can see more of the outside than I can. He starts the engine, calls the tower for permission, and taxis to runway 27. Permission to take off, engine to 100%, rollout, afterburner deployed. At 140 knots, we bring the nose up, and at 170, we rotate. We circle east towards the ocean, where we can maneuver the aircraft with few restrictions, and in literally less than a minute, we are at 15,500 ft.

In the skies of Delaware with clearance from Giant Killer

"Your airplane!" Joe says.

"OK," I suggest, "let's start with steep turns at 330 knots and then do the same at a higher speed." I make a 90° left turn and pull 2 to 3 G max before the MiG begins to vibrate. The Angle of Attack indicator points to just 12½ units. Just to confirm, I release pressure, and the vibrations die down. "Wow, is that one of the 21's flaws, my rustic proficiency, or just my imagination?" I sway into a right turn and experience the same results. It may have limited maneuverability at low speeds, I note. Later, Joe would tell me that while doing a slow barrel roll, the 21 vibrates in the apparent imminent stall throughout. We increase the speed to 550 knots. I level off, bring the nose up a few degrees, and execute an aileron roll. With the lightest of touch on the stick, the MiG drills around its longitudinal axis and shoots out like a dart. We level off again and speed up with the afterburner deployed. At speeds between 0.92 to 0.95 Mach, the controls stiffen and become almost inoperative as the aircraft passes through the transonic zone. This is where a supersonic pilot should be cautious in high-speed maneuvers. An entry into a split S, for example, must be executed at especially low speed since the nosedive part of the maneuver can bring the aircraft into the transonic zone just at the critical point when you need to recover by pulling up and away from the ground. The likelihood of making a recovery while in transonic speed is very low.

The outcome when the aircraft is too close to the ground is not pretty. According to the MiG's crudely translated manual, the absolute minimum altitude (bottom of the chart) required for performing a Split S is 6,450 ft (17,000 to 20,000 ft in training) when entry speed is limited to below 325 knots. G pulls during the maneuver are limited to 3 to 4.

Joe Gano (right) and I, after an exhausting but gratifying flight

At high altitudes and supersonic speeds, the performance is even worse.

"Have you ever done a rudder roll?" Joe asks. "Let me show you," he says and goes right into it. Although the maneuver is quite straightforward - pitch up and full rudder - the aircraft rolls violently, like a trapped beast. Thanks to its tremendous engine prevent us from entering a tall or unintentional spin.

Next, I'm interested in taking the MiG into a stall We reduce power to 60% or so and pull the nose up. At 160 knots, the MiG begins to vibrate, and at 140, it stalls. To recover, I ease the stick foreword, increase speed and power, and then pull up to a straight and level attitude. The MiG stalls quite gently and predictably and loses some 3,000 ft in recovery. By now, we have used up some 1,500 liters (approx. 350 gallons), with more than 600 liters remaining to take us home safely.

As exhilarating as the experience was, I'm almost exhausted, and my entire body cheers as we pick a 270° heading towards the airport. We start losing altitude and request permission for a low pass over Runway 27. Landing is quite tricky in any delta-wing aircraft, as a ground loop could be fatal. To compensate for this handicap, the MiG-21 was designed with quite a massive and widely spread landing gear apparatus. Joe takes over as we approach the airport. Maintaining 330 knots, we make an over-pass at 1,500 ft with a 30° left turn back to downwind 27. We reduce the speed to 240, drop the gear, and bleed the speed down to 200 as we enter the base. Flaps half down, we turn into final. Joe drops the remaining flaps and *talks* the aircraft down to 175 -180 knots, reaching the touchdown spot to rotate at 160. We taxi to the hangar and shut the engine down. In less than 45 minutes of flight, we've used up some 1,800 liters of fuel and a lot of perspiration!

I remain in the cockpit for a minute or so longer, trying to digest that awesome experience. I'm now determined to find out how the 21's powerful engine and its limited maneuverability at slow speed and range influenced its performance in real-time combat...

A few weeks have passed since my initial flight on the MiG. I am sitting around the kitchen table of Colonel Giora (Epstein) Even and his charming wife, Sarah, in a pleasant Tel Aviv suburb. The house is unassuming yet warm and welcoming. There are model aircraft everywhere, and a large painting of an Israel Air Force (IAF) IAI Nesher, tail number 561, and two Egyptian MiG-2ls engaged in a dogfight. Epstein is pouring coffee and being a little heavy-handed with the milk.

Colonel Epstein (now Brigadier-General) was introduced to me by a friend years ago when he heard I was working on this story. And what an introduction it turned out to be. Because not only is Epstein the world's Ace of Aces, with more kills than anyone else in the jet fighter era, but also a decent individual, I'm honored to be his friend and so privileged to run this MiG-21 test and comparisons.

In the late 1950s, when he was first enlisted in service, Epstein planned to join the Air Force. He was sent to take the IAF's rigorous tests and medicals but flunked the latter due to a mild heart condition. Motivated as he was, he volunteered to be a paratrooper instead and finished his service with over 600 jumps. At age twenty-five, three years after he'd been discharged, Epstein decided to give the Air Force another try. This time, the IAF chief medical examiner agreed to allow him to join flight school under the condition that, if he were successful, he would serve as a helicopter pilot. Epstein agreed. Two years later, he earned his wings with flying colors and was sent to a helicopter unit. Although he excelled there, too, he wasn't fully satisfied. He still dreamed of being a fighter pilot. He sought the opinion of a USAF cardiologist and was deemed fit for air combat under USAF rules. Armed with this opinion and a letter from the IAF chief examiner, Epstein showed up at Headquarters and submitted his demand for transfer to then-lAF Chief Ezer Weitzman. He gave Weitzman an ultimatum: "You either send me to an air combat squadron, or you send me to prison for insubordination, but I'm not leaving until you make a choice. I'll be waiting right outside your office." Several hours later,.Weitzman appeared at the door with the words: "You're to leave immediately for O.T.U. at squadron 113-508!"

Epstein's career was paved with many more such ultimatums. Although the IAF can boast 38 Aces with 687 combined kills, Epstein turned out to be the Air Force's most revered fighter pilot and legendary as both a superb pilot and a fierce fighter. Of course, at home, he happily does the laundry, washes the dishes, and babysits for his two granddaughters. .

We spent many hours in Tel Aviv and back in New York, and of the many anecdotes he shared with me, I will relate one air battle that taught me so much about the MiG-21 and about the ability of men to tap into their resources and out-perform them all.

An Account of the Ace of Aces

When the 1973 Yom Kippur War erupted, I was serving as Sector Head at IAF Headquarters while flying as an "emergency attend" at Squadron 101, the only squadron with mixed Mirage IIIC and IAI Nesher fighters. I was already an experienced pilot with some serious action under my belt, including the Six-Day War, the war of Attrition, and quite a few scrambles here and there. Given a choice, I would rather be at the squadron on those critical days.

In the early days of the war, Headquarters looked like a beehive, with people arriving and manning positions at the War Room, Communications, Intelligence, and Air Control. I was not in my element, and there was no way I would spend this war behind a desk. Things got heated up, and I rushed to Benny Peled, the IAF Commander in Chief, and gave him an ultimatum: "You either send me back to my squadron, or I'm going there anyway." He let me go. I hopped into my old Air Force-issue Deux Chevaux (French for "two horses") and raced it like a Mustang to my airbase. From there, I was taken to an airbase on the Sinai.

It is now three days since I arrived, and I found things hectic but organized. I was looking forward to getting scrambled and got my share almost immediately. It's zero-nine hours, and I slip into my G-suit, grab my helmet, and rush to the briefing room, where sorties are handed out. I am to lead a quartet this afternoon and hold on standby in the den-field phone in the cockpit. By noon, armament orders have been sent down to the dens, and we are briefed by the squadron's commander and our intelligence officer on the situation on the battlefields and in the sky. Things do not sound so good. We pick up our charts and are driven to the aircraft.

I am assigned aircraft 561, a Nesher on loan from Squadron 113. The airplane is black with soot it picked up when flown through the fire and smoke of a burning MiG-17, shot down by another pilot. I get filthy each time I touch it. I walk around the plane for my visual check as my footsteps echo inside the giant dome of the den. Two drop tanks and two air-to-air missiles are attached to the wings. I think back to flying with the AIM-9H Sidewinders under my wings not too long ago. That missile gave me a lot of grief and much 'practice' shooting my cannons in real-time combat.

Each time we dumped our drop tanks, and the wings sprang, the missiles' warheads would snap off, rendering them useless (Later Sidewinder models and the Israeli-made Shafrir II were a great improvement). I note the strong odor of jet fuel in the air and climb up the ladder, handing my helmet to the mechanic on standby. I slip into the cockpit and strap in, plug my G-suit hose, put on the helmet, and connect my oxygen tube. I will be sitting in the cockpit until our controller calls with the sendoff order and coordinates. I take a deep breath off my oxygen mask while a mechanic helps me plug the communication cord and removes safety pins from my ejection seat. The signal comes in. A call from the controller on the field phone describing targets and locations brings me back to myself in a hurry. I turn the Master Switch on, and everything comes alive. Needles are moving to their initial positions like sprint runners to the starting line, gyros humming, and warning lights flashing all around. I feel a sense of security and warmth at the familiar sights, sounds, and scents of the cockpit. The den's echoes are muffled as I close the canopy, signal the mechanic, and start the engine. The engine shrieks with increasing intensity to deafening levels while the smell of burned fuel creeps from behind. I wave at the mesmerized eyes of the ground crew and release the brakes, taxiing into the bright light of the sun. I am snug in the cockpit, surveying my instruments, inputting data, and watching the flickering lights, as I've done hundreds of times before. I feel every bump and movement of the taxiing aircraft. I have become a part of the surrounding metal, glass, and plastics. The plane has become an extension of my own body. We are one.

I notice my Number Two and the rest of my quartet merge into the taxiway as we keep the radio silent. We taxi towards the end of Runway 27, where we will begin our rollout. Although the temperatures are not the usual desert-scorching highs, it's quite warm inside the cockpit, and the anticipation is even higher. I may never return from this mission. My wife and kids may never see me again. But I deal with that fact the way I do with any other data - I push the thoughts away. I have no fear, never had. I have known no fear since childhood; of course, the absence of this built-in alert is a flaw, and I attempt to compensate for it with an intense focus on my skills and with an uncompromising knowledge of my equipment.

We line up on the runway while revving our engines and take off with a thundering roar. Forming an orderly formation, we turn slightly left to approximately 230° heading, toward the Great Bitter Lake, about halfway south of the Suez Canal.

Today is Saturday, October 20th, fourteen days since the war has begun and my third day back from Headquarters. My wife and kids are still with my parents. They went there for the Holiday and stayed after the war broke out. It's a beautiful late afternoon. The sky is blue, with moderate temperatures on the ground and visibility as far as the eye can see. I just managed to escape a deskjob, and my spirit is high. I'm back at mysquad ron, and I already have four Sukhoi kills to my credit from yesterday's scramble. Psychologically, I'm all set for more action.

We arrive at the lake but see no enemy planes. Control insists that they are there. I can usually spot bogies from a great distance. So much so that the USAF wanted to examine my eyes. We sent them some medical information from my file but never followed up on it. Ah, here they are. I spot a pair of MiG-21 about twenty-four miles away, southwest of the lake. They are cruising north at about 20,000 ft of altitude, northwest of us. I announce, "bogies in sight," lift the cover, and throw the weapons-activation switch up while unfolding the gun's trigger on the stick to its ready position. I dump my drop tanks, break to the right toward them, and glance to verify that the others in my formation are following suit. As I lead towards the rear of the cruising MiGs, the horizon is suddenly filled with approaching MiG-21s - ten or twelve pairs - maneuvering into combat positions against the four of us. It's a trap. The single pair was the bait, and the sharks were hiding down below. We simply didn't see them, and neither did Air One.

The MiG-21 has a tremendous climb rate at a constant speed, which I knew well before the 1967 Six-Day War. An Iraqi pilot had defected and flown his MiG-21 to our base. The Air Force scrutinized the plane, and IAF test pilot Danny Shapira demonstrated the MiG's ability to climb rapidly while our Mirages were lagging.

As I go after Number Two of the 'baiting pair' and blow him with a missile, I hear my own Number Two, Edres, report that he's leaving the formation to take on another pair; I continue to chase the leader, who tries hard to outmaneuver me.

Edres makes a sharp right turn to position himself well within his missile's optimum tracking angle and launches. Due to the sharp turn, his Shatrir missile passes close to the fuselage, which emits blazing rocket fumes into his engine's air intake and causes a compressor stall. His victim, though, is eliminated. I order Edres to leave for home. As I am maneuvering behind my own prey, I see Geva, another one of my pilots, chasing a MiG into the distance. He shoots it down but goes after it so far that he can't find his way back to the combat arena and returns home.

For three to four minutes, I'm still after the leader, who turned out to be the ambush planner. He's trying to evade me using every maneuver in the book: loops, inverted flights, sharp turns, split Ss, rolls, and whatnot. I'm right behind him, pulling Gs that would knock a rock unconscious. Meanwhile, the fourth Mirage in our foursome reports his own kill. He has run out of fuel and has also returned home. The chase brings the two of us to less than 3,000 feet, and that crazy pilot attempts his craziest maneuver yet. At that low altitude, he pulls a Split S, makes half a roll onto his back, and pulls back toward the ground. Slowing the aircraft with everything he's got, he is hoping to recover before he hits the ground.

Nesher 561 IAF Museum

Quick glances outside the cockpit and at the altimeter help me decide not to follow this dangerous move, and I break to the left and down to cut him off at the exit (presuming he survives the stunt). I watch him exiting the Sat zero altitudes, raising a huge cloud of dust. At first, I'm sure he crashed, but seconds later, he emerges majesticalily from his own dust cloud, at an almost vertical attitude, shooting out a huge column of fire from its fully deployed backburner. But he's too slow at the exit, and that's when I get him with a short burst of my cannons. I feel for the man. He was a fighter. My heart misses a beat when I swing back and discover a 21 riding my tail and nine more all around.

The IAI Nesher is almost a virtual copy of the French Mirage IIIC. It is a delta wing intercept and ground support fighter manufactured by Israel Aircraft Industry. With 11,023 pounds of thrust and a weight of 15,763 lbs. (0.699 T /W ratio) the Nesher is twice supersonic with maximum speed of 1,460 MPH and excellent wing loading of approximately 48 lbs./SF. It is armed with two 30mm cannons and two IAI Shafrir II air-to-air missiles. Its maximum service ceiling is 55,800 ft.

We started with a one-to-six ratio, and now it's me, on my own, against the ten of them. And they're waiting for me to get myself into one of their sights. "No way, Hussein," I grumble. "I'll fight you all. One MiG at a time." I'm excited and alert as adrenalin streams into my blood to every part of me. Eyes wide open and taking short breaths, I scan the sky for my prey. I know that with their inferior Atoll AA-2 missiles, they'll have to line up within 11° of my six o'clock to get me Fortunately, this can only be done one at a time. I'm in a defensive mode, letting them get behind me but looking for an opportunity to swiftly reverse positions. My angle-of-attack warning lights show solid red as I perform endless maneuvers at very slow speeds. I shake the one at my tail with a sharp break and turn towards another, finding myself face-to-face with two new MiGs. They simultaneously launch missiles at me and buzz a couple of feet above my head. All that's left for me to do is instinctively dunk inside the cockpit. I know the Atolls haven't the least chance of exploding at that close a range - and never head-on - but I'm still concerned about damage to my canopy by a direct hit. The excitement of battle fills the airwaves. Everyone in the War Room, at the Squadron, Operations, and on the frequency is listening in. Announcements of kills, warnings, reports, directions, and guidance are heard almost constantly. I look behind to find the next pair. Its leader is on my tail, with his Number Two following right behind. I break sharply to the left and begin a slow barrel roll, delicately pulling my throttlie back as I squeeze my thumb on the speed-brake switch and stick and stick and rudder in a coordinated roll, letting him pass. I end the roll behind him and right on his tail, then bring him between my diamonds and squeeze. The MiG explodes so close that fragments of its fuselage fly by from all directions. I look behind and notice that, with the exception of one last pair, there are no other MiGs in sight. They enter, and I break to the right. They turn away and pull up. I pull up after them. When I am perpendicular, I take my shot and hit Number Two at his cockpit. The pilot does not eject.

At that point, his Number One decides to run. I turn towards him at an ideal angle and launch.

The missile passes right underneath him without exploding. "I don't believe it!" I mutter, "They didn't give me one of those ancient 9Hs?" I'll never find out what happened to that missile, but I missed the fifth kill in that battle. I have 800 liters and 30 shells in each cannon - sufficient for a couple more local dogfights but not near enough for a long chase at a 350-liter per-minute burn rate. So, I let him go. The radio is now silent. I call Control and report sufficient fuel and ammunition for additional targets. The crisp voice of the controller comes back: "No targets in the air. Return to base." The sun begins to set on the western horizon, painting a backdrop of purple and gray up above. I cruise towards the airbase,. land, and then taxi back to my den. I shut down the engine, turn the switches off, release my harness, and open the canopy to the breeze of the open air. My G-suit is soaking-wet with perspiration. Any attempts to stand up failed. My legs refuse to respond to my brain's command, spent from the intense physical stress of battle. I glance at the G-meter to find both needles stuck at the very end of each scale-way beyond their limits. The crew lifts me up and carries me down the ladder and into the small office.

Peled is waiting on the phone. "Well," he exclaims, "have you had enough?" and adds, "Bring yourself back to Headquarters. We need you here." Since, by now, I have more kills than anyone else in the Air Force, I can't very well protest.

A couple of hours later, I find myself in the War Room at Headquarters. The large room is full of colleagues and fellow officers, and to my horror, Peled rushes to greet me with hugs and kisses. Very embarrassing.

I rejoined my squadron a couple of days later for twenty-four hours and landed myself another scramble-adding three more MiG-21s to my name. Those were the last days of the war, and all in all, between October 18th and October 24th, I was credited with twelve kills of enemy planes. Seven of them were MiG-21s. My total kill of enemy planes now reached seventeen.

Judging from my conversations with Epstein and my own first-hand experience, it's clear that the MiG-21 has limited maneuverability at low speeds. What is unclear is how one Egyptian pilot could successfully recover from a Split S maneuver in less than half the minimum altitude set by the manufacturer--contradicting everything published about the aircraft, including its own Russian manual. This is going to be the subject of my next couple of test flights.

We are taking off in a few minutes, and I am determined to familiarize myself thoroughly with all the instruments and their positions in the cockpit before we're off to our experiment. I sit comfortably and take the time to get strapped in snugly and get the oxygen mask and voice-activated intercom to operate properly. Last night, we decided that Joe would fly the maneuver and that I would be reading the numbers. I am well-rested and eager to start. It is 09:25 hours.

ATIS information Charlie reports 29.89 inches and declining; temperature 75°; due point 45° ; wind 9 MPH from the southwest; sky's partly cloudy with 10 miles visibility in a haze.

"Position and hold, big guy!"

I quickly calculate that the cloud base should be at about 10,000 ft by the time we are up therenot a perfect day but still OK for the test. We will be flying with the belly drop tank attached, which means we will not be able to use the air brakes. I set the fuel gauge to 2600 liters, the altimeter to the 70 ft field elevation, and reset the G meter to zero.

Our task is to match, beat, or get as close as possible to the Egyptian pilot's low-altitude Split S maneuver. Yet, we'll be starting off with a few handicaps. The biggest of them is our 18,000 ft safety entry altitude, which is bound to compromise performance. To level the playing field, I followed Dave Cannavo's simple rule of thumb that relies largely on the principles of converting Indicated Air Speed to True Air Speed. He factors a 2% reduction rate in density for every 1000 ft in altitude over the median altitude flown, i.e., air density at 18,000 ft would be 21% lesser than that at 3,000 ft hence maneuvering performance (at the higher altitude would be 21% less efficient.)

With 100% power and afterburner deployed; Joe starts the engine, and we are taxiing to runway 27. "Wilmington tower experimental 1165 permission to take off runway two seven," Joe calls. "Position and hold," answer the tower, followed by, "You may take off, big guy! Watch for traffic on your right." With full power, afterburner deployed, and Joe's cheers, we accelerate to 140 knots. We rotate at 170 and are up in the air within seconds. Gear up, and we make a sharp left turn towards the ocean. At a climb rate exceeding 22,000 fpm, we leave th,e area at 5,000 and arrive at 15,500 ft within a fraction of a minute. Joe contacts Giant Killer, the U.S. Navy Control Center, as we enter the Warning Area over the ocean and report our intention to exercise maneuvers within the WA and up to 18,000 ft. We level off at 18,000 ft and immediately make the first attempt at a Split-5. We are using two ships sailing below as a reference. We slow to 240 knots, roll over and pull+/- 3 g, recovering at an embarrassing 9500 ft and 400 knots.

"O.K." I'm thinking, "a grand rehearsal?" Neither of us comments as we climb back upstairs. This time we level off at 17,800 ft pull back to idl,e, and slow to 210 knots. We pitch up 10°, slow further to 200 knots, and roll 180° It already feels good. "Entry at 200 knots," I call. "Pull, pull." I encourage Joe. "Seventeen thousand feet... Sixteen thousand... Five G... Vertical ten thousand feet per minute...."

The MiG dives like an air-to-ground missile. "Angle [of attack] twenty-eight degrees... Two fifty.... Fourteen thousand... vertical thirteen... two eighty knots... four G..." I keep reading the numbers.

"Come on, Joe, pull, pull harder," I'm thinking. "Eleven five hundred... three hundred knots... vertical speed six thousand... Five Gs... The angle of attack in the red... Eleven thousand... Ten Five... Ten three... Ten two... Level off... Zero vertical... That's it!" The night before, we figured out that if we hit 7,000 feet in loss of altitude, it would extrapolate to 3,000 ft at low altitude. "Seven Thousand Six Hundred feet, pretty damn close !"

But we were wrong. Using Dave's formula should shave 1,600 feet off the actual performance. If we had entered with 180 knots, it would justify shaving off another 350 ft. We could also have pushed the envelope further by pulling as much as 8 Gs (the maximum operating g-load for this craft) and shaving another 2000 ft (provided we remained conscious).

Of course, if you do the math, that leaves us 650 feet below the ocean surface, which is to say, I'm glad we didn't try this at 3000 ft.

I play with the numbers and think of that Egyptian pilot on our way back to the airport and all the way home. I'm bothered by the fact that the numbers do not work. More for the Egyptian pilot than for myself. I am convinced that following the aircraft manual, recovery from a Split-S maneuver couldn't be performed in twice the 3,000 feet. But is the manual *ultra-conservative* by design? How else could the MiG-21 have measured up against other western fighters of its era? Even if the Egyptian pilot had understood and utilized all the margins outside of the envelope, he still needed to muster all of his own skills and some superhuman resources to help him endure the emotional and physical stress of achieving it. Of course, this was also a man who made a tactical mistake that would ultimately cost him his life, one that Epstein understood and took advantage of to bring that duel to a conclusion.

That night I figured there were no simple explanations. Were the two warriors able to unleash preternatural powers to overcome the impossible? I'll never know.

This article was first published in Aviation Week and Space Technology online magazine, EEA Warbirds Magazine, and AOPA online. Then the script was adopted for History Channel/Dog Fight/ Desert Aces, a one-hour TV show.

CHAPTER THIRTEEN
MY BIRTHDAY PRESENT

Surfing the web one day, I came across a company in New Mexico offering LOA certification in some of the most popular jet training warbirds the world has ever produced. These included the CM 170 Fouga Magister, the L-39 Albatross, the T-33 T-Bird, and the Soviet MiG 15, among others. For my sixtieth birthday, I decided to give myself a treat of some forgotten moments of sheer panic. And so, I called Jet Warbird Training Center of Santa Fe, NM, for information. I told them that I was interested in sampling some of their high-performance jets from the sixties. I then reluctantly consulted my wife, who, surprisingly, approved and encouraged me to take on the idea. We planned a week off: four days in Santa Fe and three in Las Vegas. I couldn't wait!

We arrived in Santa Fe via Albuquerque the night before I arranged to meet Larry Salganek, who owns the training center. As prearranged, after a phone inquiry into my flying experience, I was to fly the Fouga first, followed by the T-Bird, and then the L-39. I would conclude my spree with the MiG on the very last day.

Foreground: 170 CM Fouga Magister; background: Albatross L-39

My first experience with a Jet was flying the Fouga Magister in the Israel Air Force (IAF). I put a good number of military training hours on this plane some years ago. The Fouga, a distinctive V-tail jet, is powered by two Turbomeca Marbor II turbojet engines (formerly known as Continental J-69s) of some 880 pounds of thrust each. It is a highly regarded jet trainer with the excellent aerobatic aptitude and superior performance at a maximum level flight speed of some 350 knots and a rate of climb exceeding 3000 fpm. The Fouga was designed in France for the French Air Force and deployed in many countries, including Finland, Belgium, and Israel (where it was even used during the 1967 Six-Day War in ground support, armed with two 7.5 mm guns and two 50 KG bombs). The Fouga is also known as Sn unit (Swallow), Zukit (Thrush), and AMIT (Advanced Multi-Mission Improved Trainer) by IAF. It was manufactured by the Finnish government, Israel Aviation Industry, and by Dassault, and other French manufacturers. I remember finding the Fouga quite challenging for my then few dozen prop-hours and a total of eighteen years of life experience. So, pinning down speed and keeping altitude took some effort, never mind ending an aileron roll or an inside loop at straight and level attitudes.

On our first morning, I showed up at the airport to meet Larry, who greeted me in the lobby of Executive Aviation. A friendly and knowledgeable guy, Larry has dedicated his life to aviation and the raising of his two young children, whom he obviously adores. We began with some forty-five minutes of pre-flight briefing for the Fouga, going over the engine and aircraft characteristics, safety, manual bailout, and instrumentation. Everything sounded surprisingly familiar. We then continued to the ramp and toward the aircraft where I discovered, despite my moderate!

73- pound, five-foot ten-frame, how much I had grown over the years! It almost took a shoehorn to fit me in the cockpit's front seat. I was next amazed by how familiar the cockpit was, with most of the instruments, gauges, and switches just where I had left them. *Emergency brakes: on. Master sw;tch: on. Throttles: on idle. C L EA R.*

I push the left engine starter button and forward the starter lever alll the way. The engine starts with a shriek so familiar it sends goosebumps down my spine. The engine temperature reaches 640 degrees. I release the starter button, let the engine rev up and start the right engine in the same sequence. *Radio: on. Avionics: on. Check A TIS. Hydraulic pressure: normal. Engines' temperatures: normal. Voltage's good. Fuel-wing tips and main: full. Flaps to 15 degrees. Permission to taxi. Note wind direction. Emergency brakes off,* and we're on our way to runway 02.

Taxing is quite simple, given the aircraft's toe brakes. With the tower's permission, we line up the runway while bringing the throttles to the full forward position. The engines rev up to 22,700 rpm, and the aircraft rushes down the runway. At 70 knots, I bring the nose slightly up, and, at 75, without much ceremony, she takes smoothly off the runway towards the skies.

Gear up. Flaps closed. Reduce rpm to 21,500. In this 28° F, clear blue winter sky, we push 3500 fpm towards the 181 000 ft limit of our VFR flight over the New Mexico desert. Santa Fe is nestled at approximately 7,000 ft in the southern range of the Rockies with some awesome mountains surrounding it (including *Georgia O'Keefe's famous Table Mountain*), rising to 11,500 ft MSL at their peaks. I first level off at 14,500. Cabin pressure is retained at a. comfortable 10,000 ft. I do some stalls, then build up the speed to 350 knots when Larry encourages me to test out the Fouga with some steep turns and aerobatics-Again, I am amazed at how familiar and easy it all is. Obviously, as Larry puts it, "enough experience will do it to you." After an hour or so of play, we callled the tower and asked for permission for touch-and-go. I reduce power to 18,000 rpm and descend to a pattern altitude of 7,500, entering downwind at approximately 200 Knots. *Open speed brakes to reduce speed to 140. Drop the gear.* Close the brakes. Speed is further reduced, and, at 120 knots, I open 15° flaps and turn onto the base extending the flaps all the way, turning to final, and lining up with the runway. *Last check of hydraulic pressure... three greens, engine temperature, and flap position.* At 105 KTAS, I continue towards the 1,000-foot mark while over the runway bringing the throttles back to idle. *Touch the mark... full throttles forward... flaps to 15... 70 knots; nose up and off we go again...* I did two more and taxied back to the ramp. What a reunion!

Lockheed T-33 Shooting Star

While my flight on the Fouga was a nostalgic journey into the past, the T-Bird, the next ship for me to sample, was a sheer display of power. The Lockheed T-33 (also known as Shooting Star, TBird, and Silver Star) is a two-place jet trainer designed by the USAF for pilots already qualified to fly propeller-driven aircraft and for combat and reconnaissance missions. The T-Bird, which was developed from the single-seat F-80 fighter interceptor, has served in more than 20 armed forces for more than 50 years since it was first issued in 1948. With almost 6,000 copies built, the T-33 is still in service in many places around the world. This big fighter, at 15,000 lbs. maximum weight, with its Allison J-33 (5400 lbs. of thrust) turbojet engine, stands 11'7" high, 37'8" long, and 37'6" at its wingspan. It has a range of 1,345 miles, over 45,000 ft of service ceiling, 455 MPH cruising speed, and 600 MPH of VNE. The pressurized cockpit is large and spacious, visibility is very good, and all instruments, gauges, and switches are within comfortable reach.

We spent about half an hour of preflight briefing and another 10 minutes or so at the cockpit, familiarizing me with the aircraft and its handling characteristics. Meanwhile, the ground crew finished fueling the aircraft with some 900 lbs. of Jet-A fuel, and we circled the ship, removing six vital safety pins and flags and storing them in a compartment made for them in the right drop tank.

We entered the cockpit of this beautiful aircraft with its Thunderbird paint job and began reading the pre-flight checklist.

The process is quite simple, but you must keep your eyes on the EGT to keep the temperature limitation within a range of 400° and 600°, That'salsotrue during flight operations. *Radio the tower. Bring flaps to 32 degrees. Taxi to the active.* I line up on runway 02 and push the throttle to the max. The rudder becomes effective quickly as the speed rapidly increases. At 90 knots, I pull the nose slightly up, and she takes off quite effortlessly. We climb to 14,000 ft, where I level off and perform some stalls. The stalls are gentle, with a minimal loss of altitude. I then increase power to 97% and pick up speed to 400 knots, heading north towards the Colorado State line. The air is very stable, with wind aloft at almost zero and outside temperature at about -17°C. At straight and level flight, I observe the T-Bird wobble, almost doing Dutch Rolls, at which time I let go of the controls momentarily, and she corrects herself instantly. To demonstrate the ship's handling capabilities, Larry asks me to make a 180-degree turn onto a power line path about half a wingspan to my right. At some 450 mph (true airspeed near 500 mph), it would take an outstanding jet of that era to do. Sure enough, at a steep 65° to 70° turn in moderate G, I manage to make it without much of a problem. The T-33 was designed just as the Soviet's MiG 15 entered the arena. Thanks to its swept wings, it had extremely agile handling capabilities at high speed. The T-33 and F-80 had to match that competence. Staying at the same speed, I try an Aileron Roll. *Nose up about 8° and quick full-left aileron.* She did it responsively and with no loss of altitude at the exit. I do a few more steep turns and other maneuvers alongside a quick glance at the fuel gauge. We had almost used up the auxiliary tanks with a full fuselage tank, or about half an hour (plus reserve) of flight time, remaining. At approximately 450 lbs. an hour, she's a worse guzzler than my old Chevy...

I verify that the VOR is indicatingthe correct "110.60" frequency for Santa Fe VORTAC and turn to a 180° heading toward Santa Fe airport, some 110 miles south. We arrive at Santa Fe-controlled space in a little over 15 minutes. Listening to ATIS, it appears that the little surface wind at takeoff shifted somewhat southward, and we request a direct approach to runway 20. From that point on, it is uneventful. Reducing power to 85% at a rate of descent of approximately 1000 fpm, we arrive at the final at approximately 130 knots, full dirty. I reduce the approach speed to 115 knots, land, and taxi back to the ramp. I open the canopy to a freezing 25° F to 27° F weather, with a lot of warmth and affection for this wonderful aircraft.

Taxing out in the L-39

Even though it is inferior in many ways when compared to the T-33 T-Bird, the Albatross L-39 is much more fun to fly. On that Sunday morning, when I am scheduled to fly the L-39 and the MiG, the weather looks somewhat iffy. The sky is overcast with some development to the southwest of the airport, though the blue sky is visible to the far northwest. The forecast predicts no precipitation for the day except for some flurries by evening. The wind is from the northwest at approximately 10 - 15 knots.

Again, I meet Larry at the lobby of Executive Aviation, and we go over the information concerning the L-39. The plane is out on the ramp, ready for us to climb in, and I am just as anxious to get started. From everything I've heard (and read) about this aircraft, it is a marvelous machine to fly. Designed and produced in Czechoslovakia, the L-39 was the advanced trainer for the Soviet Union between the early 1970s through the dissolution of the Warsaw Pact in 1999. It first flew in late 1968, and almost 3,000 units were produced and shipped to many countries, mainly in the third world (including Cuba, Iraq, Libya, Syria, and Vietnam).

Low pass over Santa Fe Airport

The L-39 is a low-wing aircraft with tandem seating, a classic all-metal airframe, and drop tanks at its wing's tips. Unlike the Fouga, which has a roughly 35-second fuell supply in inverted flight, the L-39's tip tanks do not provide any. Inverted flights and loops are, therefore, not recommended. The maximum level speed is 405 Knots with a VNE of 491 KTAS. Still, with a medium size engine of 3,800 I bs. of thrust, the L-39 climbs at a respectable rate of 4,200 fpm to a service ceiling of approximately 35,000 ft.

Depending on tank configuration, its range is between 800 nm and 945 nm on 2,160 lbs. to 3,382 lbs. of fuel to a maximum endurance of over 3.5 hours. I enter the front seat and find the cockpit to be quite large and comfortable with superb visibility all around. With the differences between East-West cultures, I expect some differences in the operation and control of the aircraft. To start the engine, you first initiate a turbo booster, known as the Sapphire 5 single-shaft turbine, that compresses air, water, and alcohol into the main engine. This makes the turbojet engine more efficient and easier to start. I strap myself in and begin with the checklist... *Emergency brakes: on. Hydraulics at zero* (The hydraulics gauge is awkwardly situated in the far back and right of you). *Fuel at main tank 800 KG (1760 lbs.). Battery: on. Avionics switch: on. C L E A R. Push the turbo booster for 5 seconds, followed by a push on the starter button until power is at approximately 5%. Radio on A TIS. Avionics set. Steps up and canopies closed. Hydraulic pressure at 29. The voltage is at 30. A/C switch on. The pressurization lever pushed forward. Clear the tower. Emergency brakes off...* and I am ready to go.

Like the British Spitfire, the brakes in the L-39 are controlled by a handle situated on the control stick-I've also seen it on some European gliders. Direction is commanded by pushing the rudder pedals all the way in the desired direction with a full stop at their neutral position. It is tricky at first, but after a short practice session, taxing is quite simple. The flap setting is selected by pushing either one of three buttons; each represents a different setting; 0°, 25°, and 44°. I select the second. We are cleared to Runway 02, and I line up and push the throttles all the way forward at 100 knots, she takes off. *Gear up. Flaps pushed to 0° position. Reduce power to 101%.* I trim the climb to about 215 knots, and she's climbing at 4,000 fpm effortlessly. This aircraft trims so well that there is almost no need for hands on the stick. The ceiling is at about 11,000 ft, and I level off at 10,000 ft heading northwest towards the blue. And here the fun begins - but not before I receive a warning from the back that I am busting the Las Alamos Restricted Area.Uh... oh. The last thing I want is a young cowboy riding an F-16 chasing my tail. I make a quick correction, and we're out of there. Meanwhile, we develop speed to about 350 knots, changing the heading to approx. 140° and maneuvering the mountain ranges at approximately 1,500 AGL.

Starting engine of L-39   Taxing back the L-39   Taxing the MiG-15

At this altitude, you do notice your speed... and it is the closest you will legally get in a jet to ridge flying in a glider. A few years ago, I took up the sport of soaring and accumulated a few hundred hours, mostly in high-performance [fiber] glass gliders. I own a DG-303 and did a little ridge flying, the most ambitious foray to date being 168 miles over Bald Eagle Ridge in the westernmost part of the Allegheny Mountains. The ridge creates lift by deflecting upward the perpendicular wind blowing against it.

The most effective part is 20 ft to 50 ft above the ridge (not with standing taller trees). Because of the strong upward ve·ctor, the pilot can increase the gravitational vector to effectively give the glider a high-speed forward motion without losing altitude. At 110 to 120 knots, everything moves very fast underneath and around you... do not try this at home. We passed Moriarty Airport, which is, for the most part, a glider airport-though in this weather, none were aloft. We started heading towards Santa Fe airport and climbed to 10,000 to perform a flair-out emergency landing exercise. In this maneuver, you bring the power to idle and fly the plane at its best glide speed, which for the L-39 is about 135 knots. We call the tower and receive permission for flair-out landing from 3,700 AGL and touch-and-go. I figured that its glide ratio must have been about 10:1 if it were to bring us to the airport within 5 miles without power at all. That's not such a bad ratio for a jet-I'd hate to think what it would be for the MiG. To put things in perspective, the glide ratio of my DG is 44:1. That would mean that if I were over the airport at the same altitude, I could land, without additional lift, at a point some 34 miles a:way. The L- 3.9 glides beautifully and handles very well, indeed. You bring her downwind at 200 knots, at 180 knots, drop the gear, and at 160 knots, push the 25° flaps position. *Turn to base, selecting the 44° button. Three greens. The fuel's still good. Hydraulics is OK. The voltage is at 30.* Turn final,and if you p·egthe airspeed to 120 knots, she will land herself on the runway. We touched down the 1000 ft mark. *Push the throttle to 103%. Gear up. Flaps up...* and off we go! We circled away from the airport and requested a low pass at 1500 AGL. A.bout three miles south of the airport, I make 1802 towards the runway descending to the assigned altitude at 250 knots. Right at the end of the runway, I make a 30° left turn into downwind while simultaneously extending the speed brakes. *180 knots. Gear down. Speed brakes closed. 160 knots. Flaps 25° extended. Turn base. Flaps 44g extended. Establish 120 knots. Checklist. Land. Brake (remember the handle on the stick!)... And taxi to the ramp.* I open the canopy and climb down with a huge grin as I shake Larry's hand.

Now, it's the MiG 15's turn. This time, my wife is also at the terminal listening to the pre-flight briefing. I could tell she wasn't keen on this one and caught her murmuring a prayer under her breath. Despite all the bad press, operationally, the MiG was a great success and a technological breakthrough of its era. With a maximum speed of 670 MPH, 51,000ft of service ceiling, and a 7,500 fpm climb rate, there were very few jet fighters (if any) matching it. Until the F-86 and Dassault's Mystere IV were introduced, the MiG 15 was a dangerous predator- in the right hands, that is. You see, it has its drawbacks: horrible handling at low speeds and a short 500 miles range.

However, it does have a huge 6,000 lbs. of thrust engine on a relatively light frame of 11,000 lbs. maximum weight. The MiG 15 was produced in large numbers, and it is estimated that some 10,000 copies were made available to the Soviet Union member nations and its satellites.

Foreground: MiG 15 at the ramp. Background: Taxng the L-39 back to the ramp

I couldn't wait to tell my old IAF friends about this. I tell Larry on the way to the plane the only opportunity they'd had to see one was between their diamonds... It was not until I got into the cockpit that I began to understand the likeness of why the MiG was often compared to Vara Panina. Vara Panina was a gypsy singer in St. Petersburg, Russia (circa 1900), who was famous for her homeliness and her heavenly voice. The back seat of the cockpit looks like an 18th-century illustration of Dr. Jekyll and Mr. Hyde's laboratory. Once you get in (if you are skinny and short enough), the instrument panel is at your face, and visibility on the ground is restricted. Prior to ejection with a *hot seat*, you'd need to bring your feet up on top of a footrest to avoid hitting the narrow passage on the way out. I was not able to do that, and in an emergency ejection, I would have, most likely, left my legs in the cockpit. The MiG takes off at 115 knots and cruises at 500. Flying it is very jittery, but maneuverability is exceptional at this speed. In action, though, it can't be an easy plane to fly.

To conclude the day, and just in time before the onset of bad weather, I took another hour of fight in the L-39, which I quickly grew to love. Not a bad birthday gift, if I may say so myself. As far as more flying, well, while in the air, please ke,ep an eye for a slick white glider marked "ME" on its tail and switch to 123.3; I'll be listening.

On Tuesday, we left for Las Vegas, but after three days in the New Mexico sky, the blackjack tables couldn't come close to the thrill I'd left in the cockpit.

This article was first published in an issue of EAA's Warbirds magazine

Some of the [better] pictures were taken by Dan Swiderski of Albuquerque, NM. Dan was a crewman on a U.S. Aircraft Carrier between 1967 and 1971. He just happened to stop by Santa Fe Airport to take some pictures of long-forgotten war birds. I thank him warmly for his contribution.

CHAPTER FOURTEEN
FLYING THE $100 HAMBURGER
AND BEYOND

Flying has its social aspect, as well. Flyers go to multiple venues to meet others. These flights are dubbed "The $100 Hamburger Lunch." The upside of these is that we discuss mostly flying, and the downside of it is that we discuss mostly flying... many spouses resent that. Yet, I did experience some great hamburgers, excellent lobsters, and tasty steaks in many locations in the U.S.A. and across the world. On a trip Across America, Victor and I were recommended, as usual, the best restaurant in town in each destination. It was the Las Vegas' L' Atalier De Joel Robuchon, at the MGM. Itooka brief look at its special menu and cracked:" Victor, you pay.... "The food was exquisite, and the wine exceptional; I had never heard of some of the unique dishes but enjoyed them thoroughly. The bill came to about $600. Of course, I paid my share. So, this was no $100 meet; it was more like $1000, but still worth it... similar experiences repeated themselves in many places around the world. There are groups and clubs organizing meets throughout the year.

The groups are usually associated with the plane they fly, but some of the venues are suggested by many meet-up websites. I personally attended many such meetings in dozens of venues, where I met many pilots that I kept in touch with over the years.

From Left to right: Meeting with Mookie in Marathon Key, Fl | With Neil Armstrong in Reno | lunch with friends in Oshkosh

I also find that many airlines (and ex-military) pilots do not have the opportunity to fly GA aircraft and miss the "sit-of-the-pants" flying. Most never flew a glider but had it on their "bucket list." So, many thrive to join GA owners in their flights around the country and the world or to participate in a $100 lunch meet.

Here are some of my many favorite venues for pilots' meets and visits (not in any order):

Key West, FL (KEYW). Marathon Key, FL (KMTH), Freeport, Bahamas (MYGF), Nassau, Bahamas (MYNN), Lakeland, FL (KLKL), Okeechobee, FL (KOBE), Naples, FL (KAPF), Daytona, FL (KDAB), Tallahassee, FL (KTLH), and other FL locations. Savanna, GA (KSAV), Myrtle Beach, SC (KMYR), Washington Dulles (KIAD), National Aviation Hall of Fame, Dayton, OH ,(KFFO), Cape May, NJ, (KWWD), Teterboro, NJ (KTEB), Martha's Vineyard, MA (KMVY), Block Island, RI (KBID), Newport, RI (KULJU), Bel Harbor, ME (KBHB) Memphis, TN (KMEM), Tulsa, OK (KTUL), Oklahoma City, OK (KOKC), New Orleans, LA (KNEW), Baton Rouge, LA (KBTR), Oshkosh, WI (KOSH), Omaha, NB (KOMA), Denver, CO (KOEN), Yellowstone/Cody, WY (KCOD), Las Vegas, NV (KHND), Reno, NV (KRNO), Flagstaff, AZ (KFLG), Sedona, AZ (KSDX), Rapid City/Mt Rushmore, SD (KRAP), Salt Lake City, UT (KSLC), Santa Fe, NM (KSAF), Sacramento, CA

(KMCC), Santa Monica, CA (KSNO). Cancun/Cozumel, Mexico (MMUN), Belize City, Belize (MZBZ), Liberia/Guanacaste, Costa Rica (MRLB}.

Dinner with family in Newport, R.I.   Lunch with friends in South Africa

These are just a few. There are hundreds of venues reachable from the U.S.A. by small GA aircraft and worth visiting, and perhaps thousands of airports to choose from.

Dinner with friends in Salt Lake City (left) and lobster lunch in Montauk (L.I), NY

In addition, there are aircraft manufacturers' safety, proficiency, and transitional courses. I attended a few and was quite impressed with the instructions, discussions, and comradery. They were all run by professionals as well as expert volunteers.

Left: In Reno Races with Giora, Rick, and John (background L-39 "Pips"),
Right: Sarah, Mary, Rick, Pip, Joe, and Giera in Willington, DE

Left: Meeting astronaut Jack Lousma in Oshkosh. Right: Meeting
our protegees in the flying graduation course in Megiddo.

CHAPTER FIFTEEN
MY WEEKEND AIRCRAFT FLOWN

L-29 Albatross, L-39 Albatross, Avcon 120 HP, Barron 58, L-19 Bird Dog, C-23, Cessna C-172, C-172RG, C-182RG, Duchess 76, AirCam, DG-303,Discus 2CT, Discus A, Discus Duo, Extra 300

Thunderbird T-33, Fouga Magister, F-35 Simulator, Grobe G-102, Grobe G-103, LS- 4, MiG-15, MiG-21, Mini-Nimbus, Mooney Ovation 3, Mustang P-51 North American Texan T-6,

Piper Cub CJ3, Piper PA-28-140 Piper PA-34-200 R-44 Robinson Helicopter

Savanah (3 points Light), Savage Cub, Schweitzer 1-25,
Schweitzer 1-26 Schweitzer 2-33, Seneca,
Tiger Moth Ventus 4, West Wind I

CHAPTER SIXTEEN
GIVING BACK

Be as a bird perched on a frail branch that she feels bending beneath her. Still, she sings away all the same, knowing she has wings.

Victor Hugo

Flying an aircraft requires in all pilots a high degree of professionalism, knowledge, and self-discipline. The additional dimension, the open space, and control introduce the new pilot to an experience that cannot be duplicated on the ground. At first, it is confusing and hard to comprehend but gradually controlling the aircraft brings a great deal of satisfaction, a sense of accomplishment, and self-appreciation. All these, in time, contribute to the novice flyer's heightened level of self-esteem and belief that he or she can accomplish complicated and outreaching tasks.

So, I founded the New Course Foundation. With that in mind, the Foundation desires to use this powerful tool to try and help unfortunate children trapped in hopeless families and environmental negativity get out of a pattern of behavior that leads them to social and personal self-distracting ends. We believe that by being able to almost instantly, elevate self-worth and self-accomplishment, we can bring hope to confused children to the extent of changing their distractive pattern of behavior and get them to seek productive means of solving problems and reach for excellence. Our tools are gliders and human interactions.

To ensure a successful program, we first identified project leaders, and we believe we were successful in recruiting the most suitable, dedicated, and motivated people. From the project director to the last gliding instructor to passionate volunteers who want to make a difference, our volunteers are highly professional, successful individuals in their fields of expertise. Through its "Wings" project, the Foundation began a pilot. The experiment was conducted in Israel, taking children from special schools and introducing them to the experience of flying. The Project is run by volunteers, mostly retired Israel Air Force personnel, and funded by the Foundation. The beneficiaries, boys and girls 16 to 18 years of age of very difficult backgrounds; many with hard criminal records, and all were engaged in various unacceptable social behaviors.

For the pilot program, with the guidance of teachers, psychologists, and counselors, we picked twelve boys and girls from a school for children with a high degree of behavioral corrective needs, an area notorious for its high crime and deteriorated lifestyle. Because of their backgrounds, all our twelve candidates were rejected by Israel Defense Force (IDF) for recruitment. Since its inception, the Project, now dubbed "Wings," recruited some 48 candidate participants annually for the ensuing ten years in operation.

The Foundation paid for every expense, including glider rentals, transportation, and food during field days. Because the Israel Civil Aviation Administration's (ICAA the equivalent of the U.S.FAA) regulations require aviation students to come with a dean criminal record and to be of at least 18 years of age, our people had to try and change the rule. The ICAA enthusiastically cooperated and obliged us with a special permit. Israel Value Added Tax (VAT) is almost 20%. We applied to the government for a special exemption and were awarded. The Israel Air force (IAF), which rulles the Israeli sky, gave us every concession we needed to be able to operate freely-sometimes at the expense of their own activities.

Each phase of the program was year long, with field activities once weekly plus class instructions during school hours. It started with a group of skeptical kids who could not understand why anyone would do anything for them. They were uncooperative, rebellious, and difficult to begin with. In fact, on the first day, one of them broke into the gliding club's petty cash box. They refused to help others with field chores and were totally disinterested in the happening.

As repeated each year, little by little, a change in attitude began to take place. As they took to the sky and were able to control their aircraft (and their destiny), they were more and more enthusiastic and cooperative. The change was profound. Reports started pouring from schools and parents of dramatic changes in the children's behavior, schoolwork, and test results. And the change was evident on the ground as well. The students began to help each other, volunteered to complete chores, and talked with respect to their instructors, teachers, counselors, and other adults in their lives. By the end of each year, IDF appointed a special liaison to deal with 'our' children. Of the first twelve, in the first year, eleven were finally accepted to serve in various branches of the Army under a special! program, and one was accepted to serve in a national service program, helping others. The IDF took on itself financing all special schooling required under the various programs. Our goal was to turn around <u>two out of ten</u> misguided children; flying itself did much more. Our volunteers attended every field day as well as dozens of meetings with school principals and educators.

Of the 480 participants over 10 years, surprisingly, some eighty percent turned a new leaf in their lives. Many are now productive adults in their own communities.

There are many ways to give back, and aviation has many ways to contribute to society, especially to the underprivileged. Angel Flights (also known as Mercy Flights) is just another important organization for our communities and nation. I humbly joined Angel Flight as a volunteer some years ago as a volunteer pilot, donating time, equipment, and costs to this worthy organization.

The following is Angel Flight's Mission Statement:

OVERVIEW

"Angel Flight Pilots Have Earned their Wings Now they're Working on the Halo."

THE MISSION

"The Mission of Angel Flight is to remove the obstacle of transportation for individuals with medical and financial needs. We will accomplish this mission by providing free air transportation to those who need it most. Angel Flight serves the community by flying patients to distant medical facilities, delivering supplies to disaster areas, and reuniting families during desperate times."

"Angel Flight is the original pilot organization that has been serving Georgia and surrounding states in the South since 1983... since 1984 it remains an independent local charitytoday."

On a daily basis for many years, we have responded to disasters on a personal level. But after the 9/11 tragedy, we were forged into a mission for a very different kind of disaster. Our unique resource of volunteer pilots enabled us to be a truly valuablle source of assistance to the relief efforts. With commercial air traffic grounded, our volunteer pilots were able to provide many valuable services in an expeditious manner. On September 12th, we received special permission from the FAA and began flying disaster relief coordinators, mental health counselors, firefighters, and rescue workers to Ground Zero and the Pentagon. Additionally, we continued the flow of blood for several states in the South. Blood samples are typically sent via commercial air transportation to test centers before they can be administered to patients. Centers from across the South called Angel Flight to transport blood samples to testing centers during this critical time. Within two weeks of the 9/11 tragedy, we coordinated over 70 missions to directly support the relief efforts and to help mitigate problems that resulted from the disaster. Under normal circumstances, Angel Flight flies patients to the medical care they need. However, the attacks our country suffered by no means normal, and we felt, in this case, we needed to fly the medical care to where the need existed .... "

"More recently, in the wake of hurricanes Katrina and Rita, and with ground transportation at a stand still, our volunteer pilots were able to provide valuable services through air transportation. Angel Flight was privileged to be a 'first responder' and fly 450 relief missions transporting life-sustaining supplies, medical equipment, and volunteer personnel into some hit areas of the disaster. We supported over 50 communities that were otherwise inaccessible by road. Just as importantly, we reunited dozens of Gulf Coast families. These missions were of critical and life-saving importance to those in the hurricane-ravaged zone. In recognition of our efforts, Angel Flight received a commendation from Governor Sonny Perdue in October 2005. Also, we were awarded the 2006 Outstanding

Achievement in Advancement of Public Benefit Flying from the National Aeronautics Association and Air Care Alliance for the Hurricane Katrina relief efforts."

VOLUNTEER PILOTS SERVING THE COMMUNITY

"Angel Flight provides transportation to needy medical patients on a non-emergency basis. Angel Flights serves as the coordinator for a pool of volunteer private pilots and non-pilots dedicated to serving the community. Working with hospitals, health care agencies, and tissue banks, Angel Flight matches private volunteer pilots willing to donate flights with needy people whose health care problems require that they travel to receive diagnostic or treatment services. Angel Flight pilots also provide transportation for donor organs and supplies."

TRIBUTES

IAF Museum

I knew Brigadier General Yaacov Turner from my days of service in the Israel Air Force (IAF). In the mid-1980s, when he retired from IAF active service and I already resided in the USA, Turner thought it was time to establish an Air Force Museum to preserve IAF's tribute to the security of the State of Israel. To advance his idea, he gave an interview with one of the nation's major newspapers. I happened to read the article and immediately contacted him and offered him the financial help he needed. Naturally, he accepted, and I proudly became a major contributor to the formation of this important institution. Today, the IAF Museum is a major tourist and aviation enthusiast attraction https://en.wikipedia.org/wiki/Israeli Air Force Museum Turner, in his eighties, still manages and heads the museum.

Operation Opera - Art

Operation Opera was an attack executed on Saddam Hussain's nuclear reactor in Iraq. To commemorate it, I agreed to sponsor a painting by the world's renowned aviation artist, Robert Taylor. All seven of the eight

participants ,(Ilan Ramon was killed in the Columbia Shuttle on reentry
to earth) in the raid signed the prints accompanying the oil painting.

www.ingramcontent.com/pod-product-compliance
Lightning Source LLC
Chambersburg PA
CBHW051200120626
46547CB00012B/1147